EDUCATION IN MUSEUMS

MUSEUMS IN EDUCATION

EDITED BY TIMOTHY AMBROSE

SCOTTISH
MUSEUMS
COUNCIL

Her Majesty's Stationery Office
Edinburgh

The Scottish Museums Council is an independent company, principally funded by the Scottish Education Department, whose purpose is to improve the quality of local museum and gallery provision in Scotland. This it endeavours to do by providing a wide range of advice, services and financial assistance to its membership.

Scottish Museums Council
County House
20-22 Torphichen Street
Edinburgh
EH3 8JB

ISBN 0 11 493373 1

Contents

Foreword

The papers in this volume were all given at a major Conference in Glasgow organised by the Scottish Museums Council in association with the Scottish Council for Educational Technology in October 1986.

They form a significant contribution to the current debate on the structure and content of the British education system. In particular they illustrate the many opportunities for collaboration between those working in all sectors of education and those working in and for our 2000 museums in Britain – museums which represent an education resource of unique importance.

As these papers make clear it is becoming more generally recognised that education should be regarded not simply as an introduction to life, but as a life-long process for all in the community. New structures have gradually been developing in recent years to support and encourage this view. They have helped to foster a belief in education and training as a continuum based on accessibility and flexibility rather than as a process characterised in popular perception by examinations and qualifications. At the same time they have created wide-ranging opportunities for those museums, sensitive to the changes in the educational market-place, to capture new audiences of all ages interested in exploring and utilizing the rich educational resources which museums have to offer. As we move,

rapidly, towards the 21st century, museums of all types are becoming more and more aware of the need to improve and promote their services to capitalise on this expanding interest.

However while there is no doubt that there are substantial opportunities for forging closer collaboration between the education sector and museums – and there are many excellent examples of existing practice cited in the following pages – the extent to which these can effectively be seized will be determined in large part by the level of investment made in museum education in the future. As speaker after speaker emphasised during the Conference, increased investment by education authorities working in partnership with local authority and independent museums is urgently required to improve the quality and extent of provision. In Scotland for example only six museums out of a total of some 400 have education officers on their establishment, and this at a time where planned curricular change in our primary and secondary schools depends more than ever before on access to first quality external resource material.

It is recognised by those advocating increased investment in education services for our museums that success will be largely due to a greater understanding and appreciation of the important role museums have to play in education. If the following papers help to improve understanding and deepen appreciation of that role, the main objective of the Scottish Museums Council's Conference on Education in Museums, Museums in Education will have been successfully achieved.

Timothy Ambrose
Acting Director
Scottish Museums Council
Edinburgh
16th March 1987

New Needs in Adult and Community Education

Lalage Bown

Lalage Bown became Professor and Director, Department of Adult and Continuing Education at Glasgow University in 1981. She worked in extra-mural education in a number of African universities from 1949 to 1980. She is a Board member of a number of key institutions involved in community and adult education in Scotland and elsewhere in the UK.

Introduction: Museums in the Community

A few weeks ago, I was conducting a historical study tour, under the auspices of my Department, in another part of the United Kingdom. One day we visited a small museum in a country town. By most of the canons, it was an example of how a museum is not supposed to be. The main collections were crowded in tight rows in flat glassed-over show-cases, while large objects were hung on the walls in half-random juxtaposition. Because the building was so small, there was hardly room for a group of people to move between the cases. The written guide was a simple duplicated leaflet, there was no professional curator and at first glance, the place might have seemed all too like one of Flinders Petrie's 'charnel-houses of murdered evidence'. There was of course no planned interaction between viewers and exhibits, there were no recorded commentaries, no videos. From the point of view of getting the public in, it would have looked like a failure in the glossy marketing sense; there was no tea-room, no shop and no car-park since the building was crammed onto the main street.

All the same, that museum had tremendous strengths. The honorary curator, who has another role as the community nurse, came in with her basket over her arm from her Saturday shopping and immediately lit the place up with her commitment and personal references and the information she had gathered from visiting scholars and adult education classes. She cheerfully unlocked a cabinet and took out two small silver Elizabethan maces, telling us they had come down in her family and that her father had gifted them to the museum; she then handed them round as if they were as ordinary as a plate of biscuits. Meanwhile, Saturday shoppers, seeing the doors open, squeezed in to say hello to her and to us and talk about some of the items on display – telling about what they knew and asking for advice and ideas about what they did not. At the same time, I gradually became aware that the requirements of scholarship had been fulfilled, with very careful labelling and cataloguing by a succession of volunteers.

My group left with the sense of having spent a rewarding time. A simple and barely resourced set of collections had given off their messages through the mediation of the curator and other members of the community, to whom the items had personal relevance and who had learned about them from reading, from their field society, from the archaeologists and geologists who came to work in the area and from more formal educational activity such as the local university's extra-mural classes.

One would wish to see such a place with better finance behind it and with some professional servicing, but not to lose its feel of being part of a community's everyday life. I have quoted it by way of introduction to my theme, because the underlying challenges which adult and community education pose to museologists are: how can ordinary people acquire a sense that they have a *stake* in a museum and how can they see museums as places of both learning and enjoyment? The challenges are of course more easily met in a small country town where many families have lived for generations than they can be in urban settings, where most members of the society have roots elsewhere – often outside Scotland or outside the UK altogether.

In discussing these challenges, I am well aware of two points. First, although my theme is about 'new' needs, there are historical precedents for most of the suggestions I can make. If one talks of attracting adults to museums by rousing their sense of wonder (the affective element in education which another author is also going to stress), one remembers the 18th century collection at the Royal Swan in London, which enticed the public with 'Adam's key of the fore and back door of the Garden of Eden'. If one mentions the vision of a community learning complex of which a museum would be a part, one remembers the writer in an Edinburgh Chartist paper of 1839, *The True Scotsman,* who proposed a plan for 'schools for the people' which would include workshops and a museum[1]. Nevertheless, I believe that the issues are now more generally recognised and more urgent, both for those of us in adult education and those of us in museum work.

Secondly, there are excellent examples of community-oriented museums in Scotland and I would not like to appear to be teaching grandmothers to suck eggs. On a different scale, the experience sticks in my mind, as firmly as that of my small country town example, of Kelvingrove at a weekend, with a concert on, while Glasgow people sit or stroll or look at armour or pictures to the sound of the organ – the car-park jammed and people playing tennis or sitting on the grass outside. Obviously, it is impossible to live in Glasgow without developing an admiration for the community-orientation of its whole museum system. But the more conscious that directors and staff are of community needs, the more, I am sure, they would agree that further effort is needed to answer my two challenges and also the challenges implied by the title of this book – particularly the second half, Museums *in* Education. How do museums reach into adult and community education?

Definitions and Positions: The Lifelong Learning Perspective

I have used the phrase 'community orientation' and this paper is about adult and community education. At this point, we must address some definitions.

Accepting the International Council of Museums definition of a museum's purposes as 'study, education and enjoyment', it is obviously necessary to look at the *dimensions* of education. My position is that education is about learning, whether in a school system or outside it and that learning may be encouraged or induced with various degrees of formality. The most formal modes of encouragement of learning are associated with schools, colleges and universities, where programmes are highly structured and controlled by a hierarchy of examinations. The least formal modes of encouragement are through social interaction – information (or misinformation) and ideas (or prejudices) passed on at the bus-stop or in the pub. In that spectrum, a museum is somewhere between – it is neither a school nor a pub; a museum director's educational objectives are more structured than those of an acquaintance in a pub, but are premised on greater autonomy for the learner than is usual in a school or college. One would call the museum's stance 'non-formal', to distinguish it from the formal position of a school and the informal, incidental position of social learning.

Because a museum opens its doors to all ages, it is well-placed to encourage *lifelong learning* and this is a concept which has once again become fashionable, since constant scientific development, rapid social changes and the appearance of new media for communication and information mean that any person 'who does not keep up-to-date is condemned to be overtaken'[2]. Education of the young cannot be seen simply as a preparation for life, since any young person will face very dramatic changes before (s)he reaches old age. The element of preparation nowadays needs to be related to teaching the young how to *continue* learning – and I suggest that the educational objectives of museum staff in contact with the young must include: *enabling the young to appreciate the museum as a learning resource available throughout their lives.* This is important, since otherwise successful educational activities involving school-children run the risk of appearing too closely associated with one period of a person's life and hence of being set aside in maturity.

Adult education is seen as 'an integral part of a global scheme for life-long education and learning'. This quotation is taken from a recommendation on adult education passed by the UNESCO General Assembly in 1976. The document includes a definition, now widely accepted, of adult education as:

'The entire body of organised educational processes, whatever the content, level and method, whether formal or otherwise – whereby persons regarded as adult by the society to which they belong develop their abilities, enrich their knowledge, improve their technical or professional qualifications and bring about changes in their attitudes or behaviour in the two-fold perspective of full personal development and independent social, economic and cultural development.'

In spite of the jargon, it gives a useful set of goals for the encouragement of learning among adults, which I hope would be helpful to museum staff. In particular, it reminds us of the need to see adult visitors to the museum as both individuals and as members of the wider society.

In Scotland, the recognition of dual educational needs has led to the concept of community education. The community education service as offered by most Scottish local authorities emerged from the Alexander Report[3] and is best explained in the words of the report. First, the Alexander Committee commented:

'(63) If the concept of education as a lifelong process is to be given reality the education of adults must be accepted as an essential component of national policy designed to deal with the pressures of change and to improve the quality of life. The view of adult education as a marginal enterprise serving the interests of a relatively small proportion of the population can no longer be justified.

(64) Learning is a basic characteristic of life and man can learn as a result of every experience he undergoes. Education is a more organised or structured form of learning, by no means always associated with an institution. Continuing education of which adult education is a part, is thus a series of learning experiences organised, structured or deliberately created by the learner or by others. It therefore covers a wide range of situations such as some forms of industrial and vocational training and retraining, the voluntary continuation of studies begun in initial education, activities undertaken for recreational purposes, the pursuit of knowledge and skills to further

the aims of specific organisations, and individual study. The impact of newspapers and the broadcasting media or the activities of pressure groups and propaganda cannot be overlooked. Often the form of continuing education is highly specific to particular groups as in the case of sports clubs and political organisations. The educational service for adults must take account of other available educational opportunities and make provision which, taken together with these other opportunities, is comprehensive and relevant and is responsive to the needs not only of individuals but of the community and of society itself.

(65) Distinctions between different aspects or fields of education are necessary for administrative purposes but it has to be recognised that they are often imprecise and arbitrary. Adult education for example merges imperceptibly with formal education in schools, colleges and universities and with the informal activities of youth clubs, community centres and voluntary organisations. Distinctions made for administrative purposes can create barriers which impede the development of education as a lifelong process. Various recent developments in initial education are removing traditional barriers and should help to foster a more widespread recognition of the continuity of education.

(66) With the very wide connotation given to education the question of values assumes greater importance. So long as education was equated with teaching and restricted to specific institutions the aims and objectives of the process, though much argued over in detail, tended to be fairly uniform and to reflect the dominant values of the society which controlled it. Society is now less

certain about the values it should uphold and tolerates a wide range. Individual freedom to question the value of established practices and institutions and to propose new forms is part of our democratic heritage. To maintain this freedom, resources should not be put at the disposal only of those who conform but ought reasonably to be made available to all for explicit educational purposes. The motives of those who provide education need not necessarily be identified with the motives of those for whom it is provided.

(67) We have used the term 'need' on several occasions and feel that it requires some definition. The term is a confusing one; we use it to indicate the gap between the present state of an individual and the more desirable one to which he aspires. This concept can be applied to a community or to society as a whole. Needs in this sense are derived from an individual's way of life and his environment. He cannot always clearly recognise them nor can they be simply identified by external observation. Their identification emerges as a result of a process of interaction involving those thought to be in need and those able to provide for its satisfaction. Nor must it be assumed that the assessment of need is a once-and-for-all matter. It must be a continuing process and in regard to adult education is an essential one if provision is to be relevant.'

The Committee identified four main aims for the education of adults:

Reaffirmation of individuality;
Effective deployment of social resources;
Fostering of a pluralist society;
Equipping persons for change and to play a more active part in shaping their own physical and social environment.

Finally it said:

'(94) At the beginning of this report, when defining terms, we said that 'Social, cultural, recreational and educational activities for adults are so interrelated that any attempt to distinguish between them or to deal with one without regard to the others would be undesirable even if it were possible'; and we adopted the term 'community education' to describe the wide spectrum of educational opportunities which these activities sponsored by a variety of statutory and voluntary agencies made available. It is our view that the aims we have proposed for adult education are practicable and achievable only if adult education is fostered and developed as an element of community education − an element which, while having characteristics and requirements specific to it, shares with the other elements common aims requiring for their accomplishment the collective resources and expertise of all the elements. The spectrum is so wide that all the parts cannot be linked in one organisation and in some cases special arrangements will have to be made for co-operation and collaboration. This may for example be the most practicable way of dealing with the overlapping interests of education departments and the departments of leisure and recreation now emerging as a result of the Local Government (Scotland) Act 1973. However, we are convinced that it will be in the best interests of the adult education service, as well as those it seeks to serve, if it is regarded and operates as part of a community education service which also embraces the youth and community service. Adult education and youth and community service already overlap and interrelate to a considerable extent; but there would be much advantage from still closer collaboration. Sections of the public hitherto virtually untouched by adult education would become more accessible and adult education would acquire valuable, committed allies in the large staff – full-time, part-time and voluntary – in the youth and community service. We have reason to believe too that the benefit would not be one-sided. The infusion of work of a more intellectual kind into the programmes of the youth and community service would we understand be welcomed by many of the workers in that service. Cross-fertilisation of ideas, methods and approaches would be of general benefit as would be the sharing and maximising of the use of resources and facilities. We therefore recommend that adult education should be regarded as an aspect of community education and should, with the youth and community service, be incorporated into a community education service.'

This is the basis on which the community education service was established, and it has seemed worth stressing since many persons outside Scotland see community education as something different, often limited to the work of community schools. In Scotland community education is, at least in theory, the vehicle for out-of-school or nonformal education in a lifelong learning framework.

The *aims* put forward by the Alexander Committee remain on the agenda and it will be seen that they and other principles current in adult and community education are similar to aims and principles current in museum work – individual choice and development, participation, involvement,

relevance to present-day experience. In both fields too, we share concern to change the images of elitism, of a mono-cultural approach, often unfortunately of dullness.

At this point, I am chiefly concerned with broad underlying *principles*, but the application of current adult education principles to *curricula* also has implications for the museum and gallery world. Attempts to understand the present lead people to ask new questions of the past, as well as to attempt to find contexts for prevailing science and technology. Concern with individual development has led adult education agencies to emphasise creative arts – hence the large number of writers' workshops and courses in both appreciation and practice of the visual arts.

These aims, principles and curricula are *all* relevant for museums wishing to develop educational links beyond schools and colleges.

The Learning Needs of Adults and the Opportunities Museums Can Offer

If the aims mentioned are accepted, the question is: how do we make them a reality? First, we have to recognise that while we attempt to see education from a lifelong perspective, there are differences between appropriate methods for facilitating learning in adults and in school children.

Hans Zetterberg says[4]: 'Adults have to be attracted to museums, they cannot be commanded there like children'. While children are not always commanded, their presence in the museum is usually due to the action of a teacher or parent or other adult. An adult who comes to a museum has usually to make a direct personal decision, choosing to come to the museum rather than to watch the television or go to a sports centre or somewhere else instead; sometimes (s)he has to participate in a group decision, as a member of a club or society, or a member of an adult education class. The autonomous choice is almost always there. It follows that a museum which wishes to offer learning facilities to adults must consciously go out to make these offers; parents will not be decanted at the door from an institutional bus in the way that their children will appear from school (although I recognise that some may come in coaches organised by tour operators).

Once in the museum, adults cannot be offered the same learning aids as are offered to children – they have a different vocabulary, a greater experience of life and are likely to be more critical. This could pose a problem for museum staff, since alternative guides, videos etc have to be prepared. Further, staff responding to adults may need different skills, since adult learners' reactions are often unpredictable. On the tour I have already referred to, one of the participants was a pillar of the RSPCA in the West of Scotland. Both I and the curator were disconcerted, at a museum designed to show authentic 19th century life, when this person threatened to report the museum for the way in which their pig was penned!

While recognising that a person's learning needs may develop and change with age, interests of young and old may be matched in through family visits. When a family party comes to a museum, each individual helps to interpret to the other and a function of community education could be to help museums to receive more family groups. On the other hand, sometimes the presence of the young may deter some adults. There are now as many persons in our society of pensionable age as there are children in school and yet that age-group is under-represented among museum visitors. Perhaps the reason is indicated in a statement by a pensioner to Alan Chadwick (whose research on museums and community education is the most substantial study I have come across[5]): 'Have done my best and enjoyed a Sunday afternoon in our museum often in days gone by, but it was mostly filled with youngsters tearing about from one room to another'. Different spaces or exhibitions may have to be arranged to attract specific age-groups, and older persons may wish to have a place to sit and contemplate where they are not surrounded by youngsters 'tearing about'. Community education works with a variety of pensioners' groups and could help to bring them back in to the museum if conditions were appropriate.

Taking into account the varying learning needs of different age-groups, it can be said that in general museums are well suited to provide opportunities to adults. First they can offer the adult learner both information and interpretation. Secondly, they can help adults to think things out for themselves, i.e. to build their own alternative or additional interpretations. Thirdly, they can offer choices from a range of interests which an adult might wish to develop. Fourthly, they can offer challenges, confronting the learner with new questions, problems and issues. Because of this, I have always seen museums as important agencies of adult and community education.

Prescriptions: Adult and Community Education in Museums

How do museums capitalise on their assets, first to promote adult and community education in museums and secondly to promote museums in adult and community education? To some extent the answers are intertwined, but I will try to deal with the two questions separately. First, how can more adult learning be consciously fostered in museums?

Obviously a good deal depends on the basic objectives of the museum, particularly its educational objectives. It is desirable for these not to be school-oriented only, but to be tied to ideas of lifelong learning and to be translated into reality in programme planning. Events and exhibitions should have different social groups and age-groups in mind – a first-class example of this is the People's Palace in Glasgow (where I personally am always drawn to the women's suffrage exhibit). In particular, one would wish to see more special exhibitions in museums relating to contemporary issues and thus stirring up argument.

Such provision depends on staff and facilities and both at the present time are limited by shortage of money, but there are ways of being creative with existing resources (and many readers will have tried them). One well-worn prescription, but which bears repeating, is training or orientation of staff. Some exposure to ideas of lifelong learning and principles of adult learning would be of use to all staff and it should be borne in mind that if an education officer is trained as a school-teacher, and the better he or she is at catering for the needs of children, the more orientation is required for that person to become involved with other age-groups.

Ideally, one would like to see special community liaison posts on museum establishments and it would certainly be useful if the kind of well-organised structures for communication between school educators and museum workers could be paralleled for communication with adult educators.

When it comes to facilities, most museums which have the space do encourage local societies with relevant interests to make use of it for meetings. Perhaps a more conscious effort could be made to bring them in. Certainly, one would like to see more adult education classes taking place in museums, although there are obviously issues of location, security and janitorial services.

One of the perennial problems relates to opening hours. People of retirement age prefer to come out in the daytime, but persons at work can only be brought in during lunch-hours or in the evenings or at weekends. Very many Scottish museums open during weekends and there have been experiments with evening opening, but still more thought could be given to the times of opening and to arranging educational activities at appropriate times for working adults.

A lifelong learning policy, interesting exhibitions, trained staff, congenial facilities, appropriate opening times, all need to be known about in the community. I would like to make two comments here. First, community education workers have a wide range of contacts among people who do not often think of coming to museums and thus could be helpful promoters of museums among potential new audiences. Secondly, there exists in Scotland an agency called

Network, which is both a broadcasting support service and a telephone referral service for adult education. It could be that when it sends out educational material in support of a broadcast series, the pack could include a flyer from some museums giving information on relevant exhibitions and also its telephone advice might include museums. Any such arrangement would have to be negotiated with Network, perhaps by the Scottish Museums Council.

Museums have to work from their established base and if one is thinking of attracting more adult learners, questions of location and distance do arise. Research has shown that most users of Scottish community education facilities come from within a radius of a mile and a half. Are there ways in which we could negotiate cheap 'cultural-passport' fares on buses, to encourage people to venture further?

The other side of the coin, however, is to ask how far museum workers can venture. That is, we must consider ways of bringing museums into adult and community education.

Prescriptions: Museums in Adult and Community Education

In adult and community education, museum outreach is essential. If we cannot achieve *The True Scotsman*'s vision of community learning complexes, at least we could think of more small exhibitions and events outside the museum walls. Mobile exhibitions may be too expensive, but small-scale activities could be manageable. In adult education, the idea is developing of walk-in centres in places where people pass in their daily lives, such as shopping centres. A few strategic exhibits in such places would enable people

to benefit who have never been to a museum and might also encourage them to come into the museum itself. Obviously this is not the way to show valuable items, but replicas or less valuable objects could be used.

In addition, adult and community education institutions ought to welcome the opportunity to mount simple exhibitions from time to time, even to develop small collections of their own. Current museum orthodoxy is against further collection and in favour of better use, but I have a suspicion that for many people and communities the experience of collection may lead to better use. It rouses curiosity, helps people to realise that there are alternative interpretations and arrangements of evidence and develops a capacity to appraise the work of established museums and galleries – perhaps leading to greater involvement in that work. Further, an object in a small community centre collection may be a rarity there, whereas it is of no particular interest in an established museum; the donor can derive a sense of pride and participation which would be lost if (s)he gave it to an institution that put it into store.

My own experience of this is admittedly a long time ago and in another environment. When I was working in university adult education in Uganda, I enlisted the help of the national museum (a very fine one, with, incidentally, a good deal of public participation) to help local groups to found their own folk museums. People who previously would have thrown artefacts aside began to develop an enthusiasm for what they might mean. The outcomes were both that the national museum gained wider interest and support and that local communities rediscovered a heritage of which they had previously been for various reasons made ashamed. The memory of this still convinces me that we should not despise the educational impact of modest participation in collecting.

Those of us in adult and community education need to be conscientised as to possibilities and both we and museum staff should be readier to take initiatives. Recently, a colleague showed me the Transactions of the Aberdeen Working Men's Natural History and Scientific Society, which flourished at the beginning of this century and I noticed that every meeting included an exhibition of microscopes and other items. We in adult education certainly need to revive this kind of tradition and museologists' guidance would be appreciated.

In a sense, however, these are all technicalities. The fundamental point relates to the first challenge I stated at the beginning of this paper: How can ordinary people gain a stake in a museum? Some answers are well-tried – the existence of organisations of Friends, the enlistment of volunteer guides. We can all probably quote examples going beyond this – the member of an adult education geology class who spends all his spare time classifying rock specimens, the local residents who help with labelling archaeological material for display in a nearby castle.

The nub of the matter is much greater public involvement in the museum – in decision-making and hence in learning about museums as educational institutions, as well as learning directly from the museum. Such involvement was advocated by Atkinson[6] as 'a positive social benefit, as something which

has never before been considered as part of the operation of a museum'. I would like to see more joint efforts by museums and community education to organise surveys of demands and interests; such surveys could be carried out by members of the public and generate ideas as to what adult learning programmes a given museum might undertake. I would also like to see more members of the public treated by museums as both learners and potential teachers; just as members of a family interpret exhibits to each other, members of the community could be enlisted to do so (this is not the same as using volunteer guides, but is an attempt to use a wider spectrum of visitors). Above all, I would like to see ways explored of *consultation* with members of the community over museum policy.

Conclusion: More Consultation, More Research

If we are to move further along the lines I have suggested, there are two conditions to be met. More collaboration is needed between museum services and adult and community education services. We need to consult each other more often and perhaps a way forward would be for the Scottish Museums Council to get together with the Scottish Community Education Council and the Scottish Institute of Adult and Continuing Education. SCEC's monthly newspaper, SCAN, could be a way of spreading information about important museum events and activities. But the main point is to keep in touch with each other.

Finally, in preparing this paper, I have been struck by the sparseness of research on relationships between museums and adult and community education, especially in

Scotland. I have mentioned Chadwick's most useful and thorough work; nothing like it has been produced in Scotland. We all have anecdotal evidence, but more research would be helpful. What is happening in the interaction of our two professions? And what more could be done?

The opportunities for adult learning which museums can offer are very great. Between us we must find ways of ensuring that these opportunities are taken up and used by learners to enhance their own lives and change or revivify their communities. It is in no one's interest for museums to be, or to seem to be, in the state described in Samuel Butler's poem

> 'Beauty crieth in an attic and
> no man regardeth.'

Sources

1. Thomas Kelly, *A History of Adult Education in Great Britain,* Liverpool University Press, 1970.

2. Paul Lengrand, *An Introduction to Lifelong Education,* UNESCO, Paris, 1970.

3. Sir K. Alexander & others, *Adult Education – the Challenge of Change,* HMSO, Edinburgh, 1975.

4. Hans L. Zetterberg, *Museums and Adult Education,* Evelyn, Adams & Mackay, London, for ICOM, 1969.

5. A. F. Chadwick, *The Role of the Museum and Art Gallery in Community Education,* University of Nottingham, Department of Adult Education, 1980.

6. Frank Atkinson, 'Presidential Address', *Museums Journal,* 72/3, Dec. 1972.

Investigative learning in the
Roman Room, Royal Museum
of Scotland, Queen Street,
Edinburgh.

Changing Needs in Schools

Gordon Kirk

Gordon Kirk has been Principal of Moray House
College of Education in Edinburgh since 1981. Prior
to this he was Head of the Education Department
of Jordanhill College, Glasgow.

Introduction

Education is undergoing very considerable
change. New approaches are being adopted
in schools and other educational institutions
in response to rapid social and technological
developments. In addition, current notions of
education and of what the public should
expect from the education service are very
different from what they once were. This
paper seeks to show how the changes that
are taking place in schools at the present
time pose new challenges and opportunities
for colleagues working in heritage
institutions. I should like to approach that
task through the following five steps:

1.   to reassert the importance of the
educational function which schools and
heritage institutions share;

2.   to show that there are certain trends of
educational thinking which heritage
institutions are uniquely placed to encourage
and exploit;

3.   to argue that contemporary approaches
to teaching and the fostering of pupils'
learning point to the necessity for involving
heritage agencies more closely in the work
of schools;

4.   to identify the advantages that flow from
a rejection of the thesis that education
equals school learning;

5.   to speculate how, in the light of 1 to 4
above, closer collaboration can be achieved
between schools and heritage institutions.

The Shared Educational Function of Schools and Heritage Institutions

While schools and heritage institutions have
their differences – the most obvious being
that attendance at the former is compulsory
– they have an important function in
common: they both are concerned to
engender interest in and to foster the
capacity to think critically and to speculate
about the human condition in all its various

manifestations, the social environment and the physical environment. People living in the modern world are heirs to a remarkable inheritance – physical, social and cultural – and one of the central aims of education must be to induct people into that inheritance, to enable them to understand it, to enjoy it, to question it, to exploit it, to protect it, to enrich it, and to exercise prudent stewardship over it. Schools and other educational agencies have a shared commitment, along with heritage institutions, to that aim. That common commitment must surely underpin the kind of collaboration this publication seeks to enhance. The irony is that, while heritage institutions represent an almost embarrassingly rich repository of resources appropriate to their task, schools are by comparison hopelessly impoverished.

Contemporary Emphases in Education

While the acceptance of that common commitment provides a basis for collaboration, I wish to argue that there are certain movements of educational opinion which strengthen the entitlement of heritage institutions to share in the work of the schools. The movements of opinion I have in mind are those which advocate certain priorities for the schools. Thus, for example, the issue of conservation is now high on the educational agenda. The continued pressure of ecologists, environmentalists, conservationists and others, has highlighted the importance of a concern for the natural environment, and drawn attention to the importance of human interdependence, of the rational and sensitive use of natural resources, of pollution, and other relevant issues, and all of these concerns are currently reflected in the school curriculum.

A second priority concerns heritage studies. It is now acknowledged, for example, that pupils should be familiar with their cultural heritage and given every encouragement to explore the history, geography, literary traditions, as well as the industrial and technological development of their own country. The Scottish Resources in Schools Project, based at Moray House College of Education in Edinburgh, is an example of a research and development project intended to help schools in this kind of work.

A third example, which is not in any way incompatible with the case for heritage studies, is multicultural education. As that term is currently understood in educational discussion, it refers to the need to ensure that young people come to understand and accept cultural and human diversity through a consideration of different cultures and social groupings over place and time.

Finally, there is evidence now of a reawakening of interest in cultural products of various kinds. Of course, aesthetic education has for many years been concerned to engage pupils in creative activity in one medium or another as a way of enabling them to order their own responses to human experience. However, aesthetic education also has a contemplative or critical dimension, in which pupils are encouraged to engage in the critical analysis of works of art that are created in different places, and different times, and are the product of different artistic traditions.

These curricular emphases – conservation and environmental studies, heritage studies, multicultural studies, and aesthetic studies – would appear to be almost deliberately created to involve heritage institutions for they all imply access to the very resources and artefacts which these institutions harbour and preserve and mediate for the public. Without implying that the curricular priorities identified are the only curricular priorities, or that heritage institutions can only support studies in these areas, it is surely worth noting how these emergent themes for priority in the school curriculum, at primary and secondary levels, are almost bound to call on the resources of heritage institutions for their effective treatment.

Changing Conceptions of Teaching and Learning

There was a time when education was seen as the passive absorption by pupils of what the teacher said, whether or not it was understood by the teacher or the pupils. That view of education as a kind of one-way transmission is thoroughly discredited. In its place there has evolved a radically different characterisation of teaching and learning. There are three features of that revised conception that are worth highlighting in the present context.

The first of these envisages the learner not as a passive recipient of information but as actively involved through investigative work in the development of his or her own skills and understandings. The most appropriate learning milieu is therefore one in which the pupil is encouraged to think, to deduce, to hypothesise, to criticise, to speculate, to evaluate, to imagine, and to create; and the most appropriate strategy for the teacher is to engage pupils in various types of enquiry which call on the whole range of investigative skills. Habitual exposure to a learning environment of that kind is thought

to foster qualities of independence, initiative, resourcefulness, and judgement. Above all, pupils learn how to learn and are therefore more appropriately prepared for survival in a complex and changing society.

The second relevant feature of what is frequently described as the 'progressive consensus' in education is that pupils learn best when they move at a pace appropriate to their rate of learning rather than one dictated by the 'average' pupil. Everyone knows that pupils learn at different rates and it seems sensible therefore to create educational contexts in which pupils can move at an amenable pace rather than one in which they are marched at a uniform rate over the same rough terrain. It is important to note that the principle of self-pacing does not imply that there is a limit to what pupils will be capable of achieving; all that is implied is that, since pupils are likely to vary in the speed at which they complete learning tasks, it is folly as well as unjust to expect them to progress uniformly. The corollary is obvious: steps are required to ensure that what must be learned is carefully structured to ensure that progress can be made, however slowly, along a properly sequenced and graded series of learning tasks. That is, the time taken to complete a task is likely to be elongated by the need to clarify and correct misunderstandings as they occur in order to maximise the prospects of successful learning.

A third feature concerns choice. Choice in education is frequently criticised on the grounds that schools ought not to be places where pupils sit around participating only when the spirit moves them. The principle of choice in education may be defended by insisting that, within the curricular framework set by the school, there ought to be opportunities for pupils to 'negotiate' areas of investigation, to determine which aspects of a topic should be focused upon rather than others, to pursue some goals rather than others, and all of this without implying that educational mayhem has broken out. On this view, provision is made for pupil choice out of a concern to strengthen motivation and to make pupils more active partners in their own education.

These three principles of progressive education – enquiry, self-pacing and choice – have one very important implication: they each presuppose the existence of adequate learning resources. Pupils cannot investigate unless they have access to appropriate resource materials and evidence; they cannot move at a pace appropriate to their rate of learning unless a plentiful supply of graded resource materials is available; and they cannot exercise choice unless alternative possibilities for learning are created. Indeed, it is arguable that insufficient headway has been made with regard to the implementation of the three principles mentioned precisely because schools lack the necessary resources. By contrast, heritage institutions constitute a rich storehouse of resources, of evidence, of sources, and of artefacts, well capable of sustaining the kind of teaching and learning that modern education requires. Besides, the resources held by heritage institutions are vivid, immediate and real. As such, they are capable of making a powerful impact on learners and of constituting a stimulating and generative focus for pupils' thinking, imagining, investigating and creating. Far from seeking to emulate such splendid resources schools need to find ways of giving their pupils more open and structured access to them.

It is necessary to stress at this point that Scottish schools are not overwhelmingly committed to the teaching and learning strategies that have been described. Indeed, the evidence suggests that, if anything, Scottish primary and secondary schools are characterised by relatively restricted and traditional approaches to teaching and learning. Thus, for example, the report by HM Inspectorate, *Learning and Teaching in Primary 4 and Primary 7* (1980)[1] showed that there was a strong tendency for teachers to adopt an over-didactic approach and to be less inclined to adopt alternative ways of bringing about learning. Subsequent reports by HM Inspectorate – *Learning and Teaching in the First Two Years of the Scottish Secondary School* (1981)[2] and *Teaching and Learning in the Senior Stages of the Scottish Secondary School* (1983)[3] – point to the same disappointing conclusion. There is in Scottish schools what might be called a pedagogical restrictiveness, a tendency to rely on the 'recitation' lesson and to under-emphasise group and individual work and other ways of promoting learning. These comments by HM Inspectorate, based on their very extensive surveys of practice in the schools, do not weaken in any way the case for the adoption of more varied and enterprising teaching and learning strategies.

Indeed, the three HM Inspectorate documents already referred to were able to make the observations they did precisely because they detected an inconsistency between accepted principles of how the education of pupils might be fostered and the teaching and learning strategies adopted in the schools. Furthermore, other documents such as *Primary Education in the Eighties* (1983)[4] and *Education 10-14 in Scotland* (1986)[5] might be described as

'Young Museum' at the
National Museums of Scotland
'Creating Creatures' Workshop.

sustained elaborations on the need for teachers to create contexts in which pupils can inquire, investigate, hypothesise and create. And it is most encouraging to detect in the curricular changes proposed for Standard Grade clear evidence of the thesis that learning is an active process involving pupils in a variety of learning contexts.

However, if it is the case that there are many schools which apparently do not adopt teaching and learning strategies which make heavy demands on resources held by heritage institutions it might be questioned why there is a need to foster the closer involvement of these institutions in the work of schools. There are two answers to that question.

First, if, as has been maintained, the teaching and learning strategies associated with the progressive consensus really are more appropriate ways of fostering pupils' skills and understandings, and if schools are prohibited from adopting these strategies because they do not appear to have the resources necessary to sustain them, then by increasing the accessibility of schools to the resources of heritage institutions perhaps schools may be encouraged to extend the range of teaching and learning strategies they deploy.

Secondly, if it transpires that Scottish teachers are so committed to didactic approaches then they are disinclined to favour alternative strategies, it must be pointed out that even these strategies need to be supported by appropriate resources. In either case, therefore, schools and their pupils have much to gain from increased access to what heritage institutions have to offer and from fuller collaboration with them. All that is being maintained is that it is no longer professionally or educationally appropriate to offer a merely book-based curriculum that is mediated by a range of subject specialists. Books undeniably constitute important educational resources but they need to be seen as one type of resource among very many others, some of which offer even greater scope for fruitful educational activity by pupils than books.

Learning in and beyond the School

The fourth step in my thesis derives directly from that assertion. Just as it is widely acknowledged that the stimulus to educational activity cannot any longer be confined to books so it is now recognised that education cannot be restricted to what is transacted within the walls of schools. Learning takes place in a multitude of contexts in varying degrees of formality: the home, the street, the supermarket, the club, the garage, the river, the hillside, the mountain, the farm – all of these provide almost unlimited scope for learning, for the practice and enhancement of skills, the enlargement of understanding and the strengthening of all kinds of dispositions. And over the years, in recognition of the importance of extending opportunities for learning, schools have endorsed the value of the visit, the environmental 'probe', the

residential experience, field work, and all kinds of extra curricular activities. These developments have multiplied the possibilities for learning; they have rendered the barrier between school and non-school more permeable; and they have sought to make the whole environment a resource for pupils' learning. Heritage institutions are part of that environment and clearly have a key role to play in opening schools to a wider range of stimuli and thus enriching the educational experience pupils encounter.

There are many advantages in locating the work of schools in this much broader educational environment. First, it rescues the schools from the sense of isolation which follows from their belief that at times they are not adequately supported by the community in their work. Secondly, as has been emphasised by John Raven in his *Opening the Primary Classroom* (1985)[6], it facilitates a whole range of social learnings because it requires pupils to interact with each other and to encounter real rather than contrived or artificial contexts for learning. Thirdly, it fosters good pupil/teacher relationships. Fourthly, it encourages collaborative learning. Fifthly, it puts a high premium on investigative and enquiry skills. Sixthly, it makes economic sense: by postulating the notion of an educative environment with a multitude of resources to stimulate and enhance pupils learning it calls for a rejection of the silly 'arm-round-the-jotter' mentality and the proprietorial approach to the learning resources of the community.

Increasing Collaboration

The final step in my argument poses an obvious question: if changing educational practices and ideas point to the need to involve heritage institutions more closely in the work of schools how is that increased involvement and collaboration to be achieved? I propose the following:

1.   Heritage institutions need to be much more aggressive in marketing what they have to offer.

2.   The role of heritage institutions and their educational possibilities need to feature more prominently in courses of initial training and in in-service courses for teachers.

3.   Closer collaboration is needed between staff of heritage institutions and staff of colleges of education so that they work more closely in the planning and delivering of initial and in-service courses.

4.   Teams of teachers and college staff need to be given time to work with staff of heritage institutions in devising, collating and distributing examples of successful ways in which the resources of heritage institutions can be exploited to enrich the work of the schools.

5.   Clearly defined targets should be identified for each of the above. Thereafter a similar conference to *Education in Museums, Museums in Education* should be organised in perhaps three years' time and an assessment taken of the extent to which we have moved towards the achievement of these objectives. If insufficient progress has been made we should be ashamed of ourselves.

Conclusion

My thesis has been that there is overwhelming evidence of changes in schools and that many of the new demands that are being imposed can be met effectively by the involvement of heritage agencies. I trust that this publication will serve as an impetus to their involvement and to an intensification of collaboration between schools and heritage institutions.

Sources

1.   Scottish Education Department, *Learning and Teaching in Primary 4 and Primary 7 (A Report by HM Inspectorate of Schools),* HMSO, 1980.

2.   Scottish Education Department, *Learning and Teaching in the First Two Years of the Scottish Secondary School (A Report by HM Inspectorate of Schools),* HMSO, 1986.

3.   Scottish Education Department, *Teaching and Learning in the Senior Stages of the Scottish Secondary School (A Report by HM Inspectorate of Schools),* HMSO, 1983.

4.   Consultative Committee on the Curriculum, *Primary Education in the Eighties,* 1983.

5.   Consultative Committee on the Curriculum, *Education 10-14 in Scotland,* 1986.

6.   J. Raven, *Opening the Primary Classroom,* Scottish Council for Research in Education, 1985.

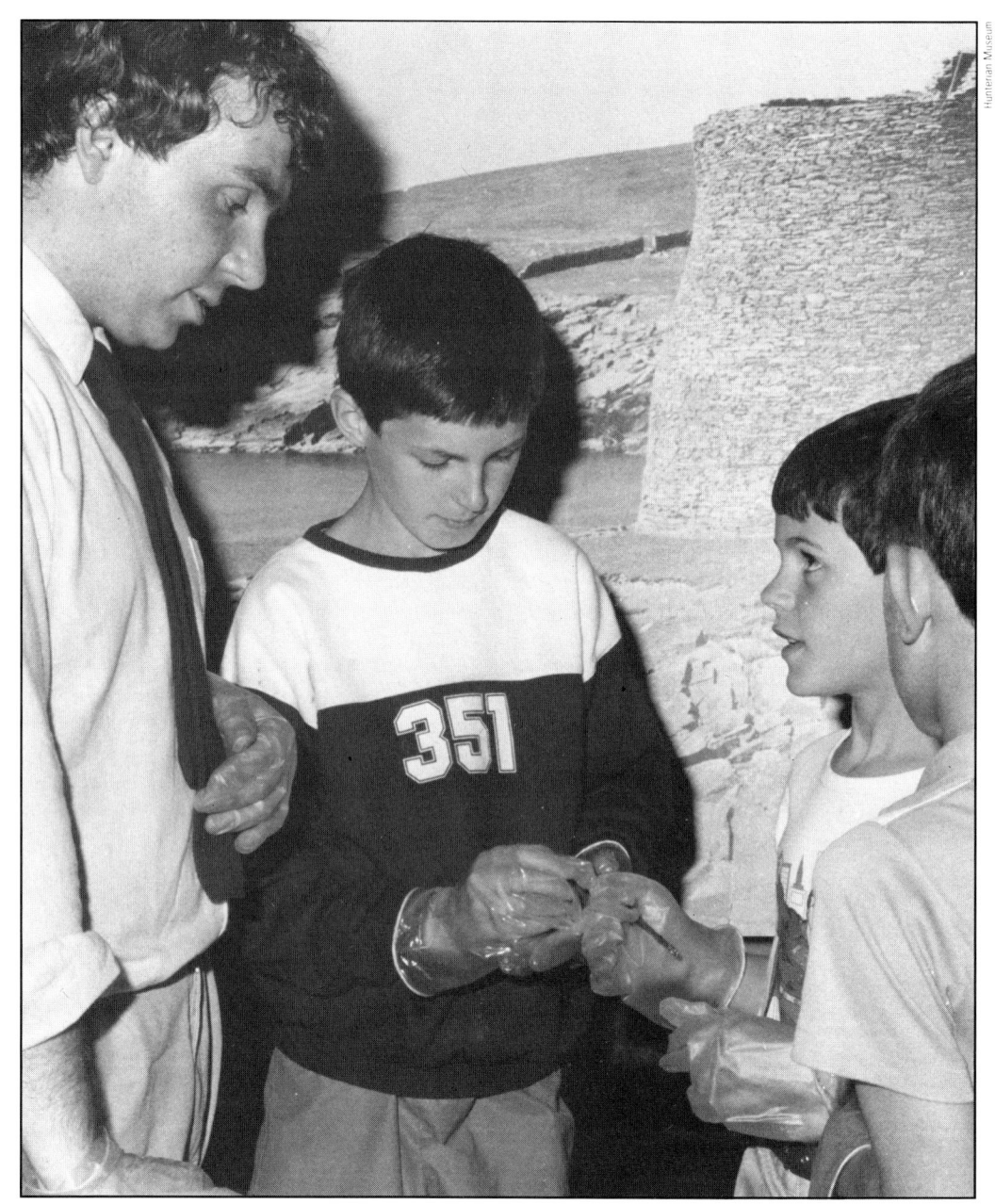

Hunterian Museum

*Handling the past at the
Hunterian Museum, University
of Glasgow.*

Museums in Education:
Seizing the Market Opportunities

Leslie Rodger

Leslie Rodger holds the Chair of Business
Organisation at Heriot-Watt University, Edinburgh.
He joined the University in 1974 following a career
of 25 years in business and has extensive
experience in international marketing. His many
publications on marketing are widely known.

Introduction

I have been invited to write about seizing market opportunities and I will, most certainly, write about market opportunities. But I will also write about other things as well – like market threats and the strengths and the weaknesses of the museum business. I call it a business. This may send shivers down some of your spines. After all, museum staff are the custodians of treasures and artefacts held in trust on behalf of the nation and your local community. What on earth – or in heaven – could this have to do with 'business'?

I make no apology for using the term. On the contrary, accepting that you are 'in business' is accepting in effect that there is a market or a number of different markets for your services and that you have to compete with other service providers to satisfy people's needs and wants. Being 'in business' may appear to imply a profit motive and what is wrong with that? But, if some of you prefer,

it should at least imply the avoidance of loss. No enterprise, and this includes museums, should be content to operate at a loss.

Perhaps the greatest obstacle museums have to overcome is their name. An article in the *Weekend Scotsman* earlier in the year asked what the word 'museum' conjured up in their readers' minds. Serried ranks of glass cases, crocodiles of hushed schoolchildren? Displays of fragmented pottery and stone? Or do people think of recent major cultural happenings – of museums as examples of cultural entrepreneurship able to mount record breaking and blockbusting events like the Emperor's Warriors Exhibition in Edinburgh, or the Burrell Art Gallery – currently the most popular tourist attraction in Scotland – or the Jorvik Viking Centre in York, or the Boat Museum at Ellesmere Port?

Marketing, if it means anything, means getting your image right and then communicating with the market place to ensure that the perceived image of your museum coincides with the reality.

The title of my paper 'Seizing market opportunities' presumes that you acknowledge the fact that – whether you like it or not – museums are fairly and squarely in the market for customers. So is any other business. You have to compete for those customers. So does any business. Such differences as may exist between your museum business and the industrial and commercial enterprises in your area have more to do with the size, scope and nature of your operations than with the philosophy of how you run your particular enterprise. Most of you in comparison with industry and commerce run relatively small businesses. But there are some pretty substantial museum businesses. Glasgow's museums already have a turnover of £6.5 million a year – a good deal bigger than that of many Scottish manufacturing companies.

But one thing that all businesses need to survive and grow is customers and this is as true for you as for any other form of enterprise. Different customers vary in what they want and take away from a museum. You have many different publics to satisfy and you have to compete with other forms of activity.

Every business – including museums – is under increasing pressure to justify its existence. Like it or not you are in competition with other forms of leisure, entertainment and educational activities:

General sightseeing

Visiting historical sites, stately homes, castles, churches and gardens

Art galleries

Craft centres

Conservation and Industrial Heritage centres

Interpretive centres and nature trails

Theme Parks

Safari Parks, Zoos, Dolphinariums and Bird Sanctuaries

Fairs and Festivals

The Performing Arts

Sport.

This is the £30 billion market-place in which you have to compete and justify your existence, your viability, your funding and your sponsorship. You are competing, if not directly in many cases for the customer's money, then certainly for the customer's time, attention and interest.

The theme of this publication is education and I will a little later on, address myself to the subject of marketing in this context. But for the moment I want to deal with the subject in rather broad terms.

Working for Customers

First and foremost, marketing is knowing and being known by your customers, existing and potential. We are all in the business of working for customers. Our job, whatever we do, is to identify, anticipate and satisfy customer needs and wants. These needs and wants are not static. They are dynamic. They constantly change. Lifestyles change, people's values change, the cultural environment changes, technology changes. We live in an era of visual media where 98% of the population have a colour TV set, when one in four households has a video recorder or a home computer – when every self-respecting infant can sing television jingles before they can recite their two-times table.

Because the environment is constantly changing, seemingly, at an ever faster rate, we, in our respective businesses or professions, have to change. For the museum world, coping with change, it is sometimes said, may come less easily than for some. After all, the museum's preoccupation is with preserving the past and recording change rather than adapting to it. In other words, the museum world has to reconcile two apparently conflicting aims – being both past-oriented and future-oriented. What does the future hold for museums and how will they cope with the need for change? Well, being more market-centred rather than museum-centred – in other words, being more marketing-oriented – is one way.

So to sum up this far. Imagine your customers are a family. Either individually or collectively as a family unit what they might be saying to you is:

'We don't know who you are'

'We don't know your ORGANISATION or what you stand for'

'We don't know what you have to offer us'

'We don't know your potential to meet our needs'

'We don't know if you even understand our needs'

NOW – What was it you wanted us to think and do?

Moral: Marketing is knowing and being known by your customers, existing and potential.

Marketing has to start out as a philosophy or attitude of mind towards the way we run our museums – a process of returning and coming to terms with what we are doing, how and why we are doing it and who we are doing it for.

Marketing is based on the concept that a satisfied customer is the most important asset that any museum can have. To win and keep a satisfied customer you have first of all to be 'visible' and here I mean being heard as well as seen. You have to be known, noticed, distinguishable and yes, perhaps even conspicuous, before anyone can decide to avail themselves of what it is you have to offer. Until you are known to a potential customer, until they know what you are about, nothing happens except by chance. Everyone has a choice to make. That choice will be based upon his or her perception of what your museum is and what it offers when compared with similar assessments of the readily available alternatives.

The object of marketing is to reduce that element of chance in the customer's decision-making process and to provide the potential customer with information, incentives and inducements on which to base a considered choice and to ensure that the wisdom of the choice was justified and enhanced through experience.

So – marketing starts with knowledge of customers (both existing and potential), their needs, aspirations, attitudes, values and expectations. Customer research is vitally important in the form of both desk research and field studies. You must also have knowledge of your competitors who cover a very wide spectrum indeed. Every museum director or curator should have a sign on his desk. 'Know thy customers and thy competitors'. Then you must design a 'total quality experience' which will attract customers to *your* museum.

Customers are people. You are in the people business. But they are not dots or digits or a grey impersonal mass 'out there'. They are individuals with varied needs both overt and below the surface, tangible and intangible, rational, emotional, educational and social. And you have to tap them at every level.

What customers buy is a 'total experience'; a package of benefits; a high quality environment that provides a stimulating, entertaining, educational experience – participatory, hands-on and interactive with a range of facilities that provides something for all the family. And if this includes shops, cafes, play-areas and crèches so be it. Cakes and ale (or lemonade) and every kind of innovatory entertainment and mode of instruction and display are all part of today's museum package of benefits and, of course, also a source of income.

This is what you have to offer – a total package of benefits – that is what the customer is looking for. That is what the customers buys – a stimulating, good value-for-money and time-spent experience whilst at the same time fulfilling an educational and informational role.

Every museum has its special characteristics and ethos, its particular strengths and weaknesses. Each museum management has to try to develop some comparative advantage, some special competence – whether it be a particular skill, resource, facility, expertise or a combination of these. This differential advantage must then be identified, related to the specific customer sectors or market segments you seek to serve and made the focus of all the communications which you send to the market. Your communication messages must then convey customer benefits which are readily understood or deducible by them.

Now you may say – this is all right if you are a manufacturer of canned soup or soap-powder, a seller of Aero chocolate bars or even aero-engines. But what has all this marketing business got to do with museums? I'll tell you what it's got to do with museums. If you don't attract the customer's time and money in the leisure, entertainment and educational market – the edu-tainment or leisure-learning market as it has been called – then someone else will.

Like any business you depend for your existence on customers. No customers – no revenue for the independents. If you rely on public-sector support, how long before lost customers gets translated into cut-backs in funding. Public funding is not going to rise in real terms in the foreseeable future. We know that already. So how to survive and grow?

The Marketing Concept
The marketing philosophy or concept sets out to do three things in the context of museums, I suggest –

1.   To heighten our awareness of and commitment to the present and emerging needs of customers in the leisure, entertainment and educational markets.

2.   To differentiate the museum experience package in ways which will give customers a basis on which to exercise a free and considered choice in our favour. We attempt to do this by applying our skills to the full range of customers' needs and expectations and by each of us doing it in our own style – in others words by differentiating our individual product/service package. We already have a basic differentiation between the scientific, industrial, maritime, fisheries,

agricultural, textiles, arts, crafts, community history and heritage.

Difficult it may be to build a differential advantage into your museum offering but by no means impossible with a little imagination and creativity. Maybe we can say that 'In the museum we design exhibits; in the market-place we sell a "quality experience"'.

3.   To influence and persuade people to prefer our 'quality experience' offering to anyone else's. And here we are back to communication – credible, consistent and professional communication. And by that I do not just mean advertising and promotion.

Marketing is not just an advertising campaign or the odd P.R. press release or leaflet distribution. It is not putting up a few posters or running a commercial or two on your local independent radio station. It is not carrying out the occasional piece of market research. Nor is it just a fancy name for selling. Still less is it to be thought of as another name for aggressive selling. If you have done your marketing properly there is no need for so-called hard-selling. Hard-selling is a consequence of *poor marketing* or doing no marketing at all.

Marketing is not just a change of title for a former museum information or public relations officer – to marketing director or marketing officer – but nothing else changes. Marketing is not a part-time occupation for museum officials with other responsibilities. Nor is marketing something to which you only pay lip-service to show that you are 'with it' and up with the modern jargon. Lip-service is the kiss of death for marketing or for anything else we

do for that matter. Marketing is not a veneer to be overlaid on the day-to-day running of your museum. It has to do with the very way in which you run your museum, its raison-d'être, your mission if you like, and the why and how of what you are doing.

Everyone in the organisation must be committed to the marketing concept from the museum director or curator and the exhibit designer to the attendant, the doorman, the person sitting at the reception or information desk and the telephone operator. A cheery voice, a welcoming smile, a helpful, knowledgeable attendant are all part of marketing – the impression you make on the visiting customer and the feeling they take away with them when they leave.

I have used one or two big words. Every profession is guilty of creating its own jargon or gobbledygook. Marketing is no exception. I have talked about product and service differentiation and market segmentation. All this means is designing the museum offerings to meet the specific needs of identified groups of customers with identical or similar interests and requirements.

The Marketing Mix
Another piece of jargon you often hear about from marketing people is the so-called 'marketing mix'.

This covers a number of controllable variables used to influence your target markets – things which you can do to influence and persuade people to act in your favour – the marketer's bag of tools, if you like. Here are the key elements:
Market Research and Assessment
Product/Service Planning and Development

Pricing
Promotion
Place
Presentation
People.

Market Research
Marketing starts with knowledge of the customer. So I put this first because this is how you find out about the customer:

Feedback. We have one mouth and two ears and they should be used in that ratio. It was Rudyard Kipling who said:

'I keep six honest serving men
(They taught me all I know)
Their names are what and why and when
And how and where and who'.

These are the tasks of market research.

How many visitors – who are they – where did they come from – what attracted them – what did they come to see – when – for what purposes – under what circumstances – with what reactions?

The means we employ to do this are:
1. Desk research (data published by other organisations such as government, research associations, specialist libraries, directories, press and journal reports, syndicated reports by independent research organisations e.g. Henley Centre for Forecasting, AGB, Taylor Nelson).

2. Observation – watching what visitors do.

3. Experimentation – changing things around and observing the effects.

4. Survey research (among customers – face-to-face in the street, on the doorstep, in the home or by mail questionnaire or telephone interview).

Market Assessment
This is or should be the result of market research. Market assessment and estimation – visitor projections by type of visitor, visitor characteristics and interests.

Here you set out to quantify as best you can the various customer groups or market segments. These break down for example into children/adults/family parties/OAP's/ tourists/local residents/organised parties from schools and colleges or special interest groups e.g. heritage societies. Then there are researchers, historians, film makers, broadcasters, press representatives, professional visitors.

Product/Service Planning and Development
Having established who your present and potential customers are – their needs and their interests – how do you plan and develop the museum product/service offering (or the 'quality experience package' I mentioned earlier)?

The customer is becoming more discriminating. Visitors today are more concerned than ever to understand and appreciate every aspect of the places they go to and the range of those interests appears to be widening all the time.

The museum package covers both hardware and software (audio-visual aids – film, slide and video-cassette guides, lectures, seminars, symposia). It covers all the other facilities – shops, merchandise, catering, play-areas, crèches etc. It takes in corporate and brand identity. If I can give you an example. The City of Edinburgh Art Centre is the corporate

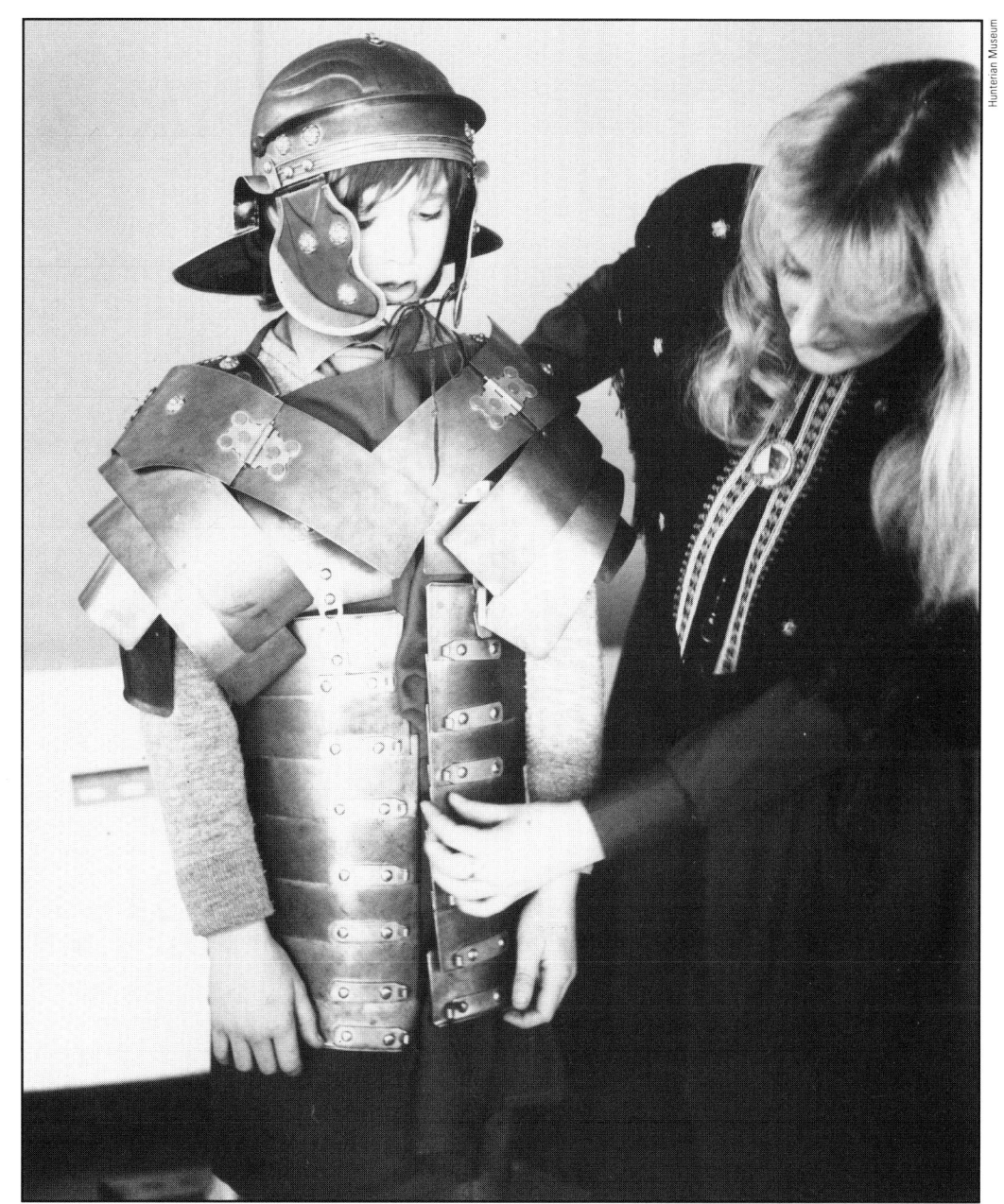

A new recruit to the Roman Army – museum education in the classroom.

identity. The *Emperor's Warriors* exhibition the Art Centre mounted in 1985 was a specific product or brand promotion.

And we have to ask ourselves:

What is the museum experience package going to be 2 years from now, 5 years from now? What is going to be the impact of the newer technologies in documentation, information storage and retrieval, word processing, desk-top publishing, printing and facsimile technology and display technology (like holography) in the years ahead?

Decisions have to be taken now and investments laid down which will determine the shape of our museums in the 21st century. The museum package is, indeed, a complex one.

Pricing
Here we are concerned with:
Levels and differentials
Discounts and concessions
Value-for-money judgements by customers.
Just as there is no such thing as a free lunch so, in my view, there is no such thing as a free museum. Somebody has to pay for it whether by admission fee at the door or by donation or subscription or sponsorship or through central and local government grant.

There is also, of course, every incentive to develop other revenue-generating activities of the kind I have been describing.

Promotion
This covers:
Personal selling
Advertising
Special promotions
Public relations.
Advertising and public relations can take

place at two levels – at the corporate level through museum councils and associations and at the individual museum level.

Place
This includes:
Location
Accessibility (this is not just a question of public transport and parking facilities but also opening hours)
Delivery systems (e.g. touring exhibitions).

Presentation
Here I am talking about the physical, tangible environment – layout, furnishings, graphic design, noise level, and the whole audio-visual experience – as well as the intangibles – the ethos, the atmosphere, the character, the goodwill.

People
Here I am referring to the people who run museums and particularly those who have direct or indirect contact with customers – the former's appearance, attitudes, behaviour, commitment, motivation and training.

If you were to ask me what marketing is all about my short answer would be – it's about all of these things and getting all of these things right. Because they are all interdependent interactive and mutually reinforcing. Miss out on any of them, get them out of balance, and the overall effectiveness of your marketing effort is diminished.

It doesn't matter how good the exhibits are if you're not made welcome or the loos are dirty, or the restaurant food and service are poor.

Marketing is about how you present

yourselves and what you have to offer to the outside world, how you communicate with it. And not just with customers. But other people who are in a position to influence your future success – funders, donators and sponsors. To gain their confidence and support you need to be and you need to be seen to be credible and realistic in your marketing thinking and planning and professional in your attitude and actions.

You need to have a marketing objective and strategy for your museum for the next 4 or 5 years at least. You need to have a formal detailed marketing plan for your museum for the year ahead or possibly the next two years covering all the areas I have been describing to you. And you need the professionally trained staff to implement your plans effectively.

But this is another story, for another publication perhaps.

Marketing Museum Education
Let me now turn to marketing in the context of the theme of this publication – museum education.

First of all, the education market is a growth market. The overall market trends are in the museum's favour.

The highly respected Henley Centre for Forecasting predicts that spending on leisure-learning activities which currently accounts for only 5% of total leisure spending should increase by 10% by the end of this decade. The Henley Centre believes that the increasing numbers of those with more time on their hands, due to shorter working lives, will seek to emulate their structured work lives by developing leisure

activities that are more disciplined and project-based. Stimulating and entertaining they must be but the emphasis will be on learning and the motivation will be educational, informational and instructional. Activity or project-based learning is demonstrably effective.

The whole thrust in our society is towards greater involvement, participation and interaction with what is going on around us. People are more discriminating. They are no longer sponges waiting around to soak up anything that is thrown at them. Wherever we look we see that activity – or project-based learning is the key to a sound educational policy. And museums are particularly well-placed, it seems to me, to capitalise on this trend.

What then are the threats that stand in the way or could stand in the way of museums fulfilling this role?

Only your own complacency and inertia, if I might be so bold. Those of you who continue to give education a low priority and low status, those of you who regard it as no more than a fringe activity, those among you who see education in terms of school parties with clip-boards and prepackaged worksheets will fail to realise your full potential. Not that I wish to imply that there are no museums which see education as their central role and their core activity. Of course there are and some do it very well. But for many it remains peripheral. If the primary function of a museum is not education (in its widest sense) then it has little reason to exist. Museums are, in a sense, the real open university of the nation with the ability to help meet both the formal and informal learning needs of all members of the community, children and adults. Community education can attract funds from the Manpower Services Commission as well as local sponsorship and educational expertise. You have the opportunity to be the cultural entrepreneurs of our society. Just as business has its entrepreneurs so you in the museum world can be entrepreneurs – in culture, in heritage and in learning – in other words to maximise the use of the museum environment.

You have the opportunity to identify and provide the leisure pursuits that undertake the project – or activity – based approach. You will have to become more adept visually and less reliant on the written word and the static exhibit. You will have to become more person-centred. You must be able to attract, excite and inspire.

You will have to rely less on lectures and notes and more on hands-on experience, workshops, letting children dress up in old clothes, handle things, operate machinery. In other words, in the design and presentation of programmes the challenge and the opportunity is to become more user-oriented.

The changing school curriculum provides opportunities for museums to work closely with teachers and children to develop resource materials held in their collections that are geared to these changes.

Recognising the opportunities in the educational market is one thing, seizing them is another.

This is where the marketing discipline can help:
To identify customer groups

To determine educational objectives
To formulate a strategy for educational activity
To develop an educational marketing programme as part of your overall marketing plan
To implement that programme using all the available marketing tools – the educational marketing mix.

The elements of the marketing mix are all ways of communicating with your potential market; of involving teachers, school groups, clubs and societies, and children and adults both as individuals and as family units.

Good communication between museums and schools at the local level are especially important in order to understand each other's requirements and to make the best use of the resources and services available. Additionally, structured visits by teachers and even placement in museums as part of teacher training programmes to gain experience of the museum environment and collections-related work are part of this communication process.

At the end of the day you have to provide the right 'quality learning experience', the right package of benefits, at the right price, in the right place and the right environment. You have to effectively advertise and promote what you are offering with up to 10% of your budget allocated for this purpose. And you have to have the right people to carry all this out. Every museum should have a full-time education or educational development officer, ideally, with training in child or educational psychology.

A tall order, maybe, but not impossible. Central and local government, business firms, trusts and foundations, individuals and institutions are open to well-argued and well-presented initiatives for enhancing the provision of community education: in a civilised society, education is an integral part of your and everyone else's social responsibility. An educated society is our greatest investment and our greatest safeguard for the future.

No business can survive and grow without investing in new plant and equipment and in a skilled workforce. Museums, as creators of wealth and contributors to our social, economic, cultural and educational development are no different in this respect. Self-help has a vital part to play in this. Not just at the local level but at the industry level if I can refer to you for the moment as the museum industry.

Institutional arrangements organised through your national and regional councils and associations, both formal and voluntary, can help here. The sort of thing I have in mind is, for example, the establishment of national and regional museum educational exchange and resource centres involving museums and schools and the broadcasting media which would act as a clearing house for ideas, materials and resources in education.

With the new school curriculum developments taking place and the creation of new local education authority posts aimed at preparing educational packages for teachers, such an initiative would be timely.

We know that the great majority of local museums are unable to provide any educational service or facilities or, if they are, this is by curatorial rather than educational staff. We know that those museums without educational staff will not suddenly be given the resources to employ them.

A recent initiative by the Scottish Museums Council seeks to develop a co-operative network of regional museum education centres and resources supported by a small central advisory staff . . . with the aim of each region possessing in the foreseeable future at least one museum education centre based at a major museum. The centrally-based staff would work with the local museums and local educational authority to develop resource materials, teaching packs, teachers' seminars etc. In other words, what a single local museum or local authority could not itself immediately afford to do might become feasible on a shared-cost basis.

Also at the regional and local level there are opportunities for establishing Heritage Enterprise Trusts involving local businesses and trade and professional associations as well as private citizens to fund or sponsor community education and heritage projects.

Every museum has its own particular strengths and weaknesses. The opportunities for differentiating the package of benefits you can offer are enormous. No two museums need to be identical. Difficult, yes. But not impossible. When it comes to the question of what makes the difference between one product and another or one museum and another, I am reminded of the fact that the woman I married is 72.8% water along with all other women. Now – just what made the difference? Whatever it was – vive la différence!

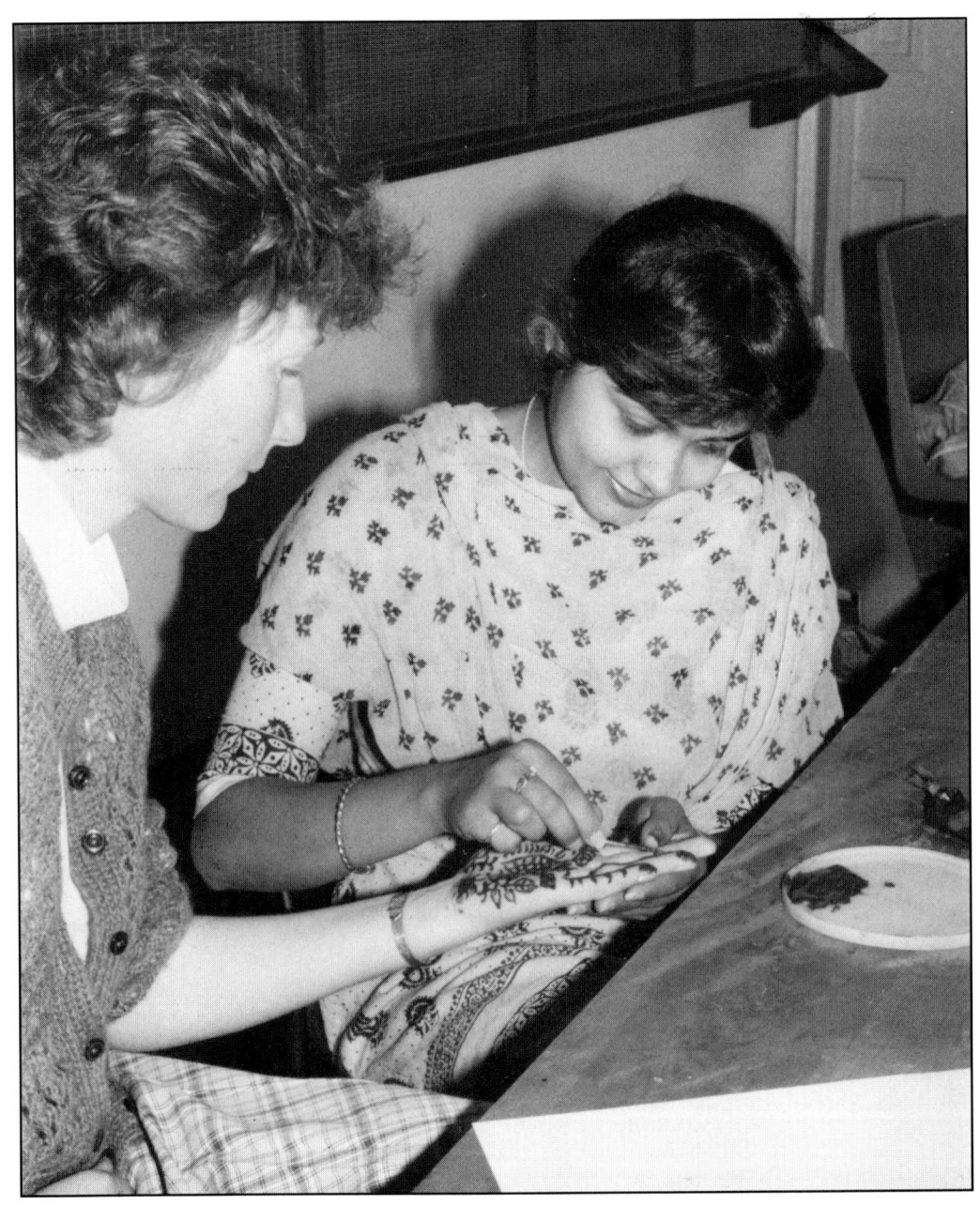

Multi-cultural work at Leicester Museum:
Indian hand-painting.

Museums in Education:
Towards the End of the Century

Eilean Hooper-Greenhill
Eilean Hooper-Greenhill joined the Department of
Museum Studies at the University of Leicester as
Lecturer in 1980, having previously been Education Officer
at the National Portrait Gallery in London.
She has published widely on museums and education.

Introduction

All of a sudden, museums are news. Nearly every day there are reports on the ethics or practicalities of charging, the problems of appointing directors who immediately resign, the surliness of warders, or the quality of the café. 'Heritage', that catch-all expression, is big business, both for home consumers and for the overseas market. A new aggressive leisure industry is emerging very fast and museums are trying to define their role within this.

Attention is also being paid by sociologists to the meanings that museums try to transmit. Museums are increasingly becoming more visible than they have been for most of this century, and investigations into museum practices and potentials are beginning to emerge from new quarters, which include both the new areas of Leisure Studies or Departments of Tourism, and the existing departments of Cultural Studies. Questions that are being asked include, 'What is the market potential for the educational visit to the museum?'[1] and 'What is the ideological base for the representation of culture in museums?'[2].

Questions are also being asked by the so-called minorities, women[3], ethnic[4] and handicapped groups[5].

These questions about traditional museum practice are coming both from within the museum field and from without, and there is no doubt that museums are shaken from their long-standing complacency and are being galvanized into action. How does museum education stand in relation to all this? This paper attempts to summarise some of the changes that are in process both in museums, and in the educational world, and to suggest some of the responses that museum education might make.

Changes in Museums

The traditional task of accumulating the sort of objects that have always been collected, such as paintings, costume, and fine furniture, is now seen to be the collection of objects that represent only one section of society[6]. Even the collection of apparently neutral natural history objects has been traced back to the collections of hunting trophies that embellished the halls of the wealthy[7]. Traditional collecting practices are now increasingly seen as the institutionalisation of the habits of those that have had power in society[8] and it is recognised that these dominant definitions of what counts as important and worthwhile do in fact privilege the privileged, in museums as in other areas of social practice[9]. Debates are in progress about what a more democractic method of collecting might consist of[10] and how this might demand new categories of material and new divisions of knowledge in the museum[11].

A second traditional function of the museum is conservation. In the past this has been carried out in order to preserve the objects for themselves. This has been seen as an end in itself. Now we are asking the question why, for what end do we preserve these objects, what are they for and how does conservation for the future relate to use in the present? The logistics of large collections and of 'museum imperialism'[12] are being analysed at all levels from many different points of view, and the conclusions that are emerging are that if we cannot keep collecting ad infinitum, we must use what we have to better advantage. A move is in progress from accumulating collections to providing services in museums. Some of us would say that the move is a little too stealthy, but none the less it can be detected, with varying degrees of evidence depending which type of museum you are looking at, and it certainly figures in all the future-oriented literature[13].

Where the needs of the visitor are taken into account in a serious and effective way, those museum practices that relate almost exclusively to the ego of the curator will have to change. The recent Buddhism exhibition at the British Museum, for example, was found to be incomprehensible to the visitor with no specialist knowledge and not at a high enough level for the academic visitor, many of whom took a different intellectual standpoint in any case[14]. Merely putting on show the sample of the collection that the curator happens to like best, or know most about, while failing to give a general introduction to the subject that the material relates to, only serves to confuse. When more than ten curators are involved and no common aims are identified, the confusion is compounded. A recent American survey, 'Museums for a New Century', stressed that in a climate of increasing financial accountability it is the museum that has built up a strong relationship with its clientele and a strong tradition of service and relevance that is surviving the best[15].

In discussing these issues, what do we collect now, and what do we do with it, we are moved to ask an even more fundamental question; what is the museum for anyway, and how does it relate to other institutions in society? And if we decide that the museum is a place where things are collected, documented, and displayed for the benefit of people, we have to ask, what is it that people want, or need, or; how can we as museologists best serve the interests of our clients, both now and in the future?

The answers to this question may lead us into some unusual areas and we may have to expand the traditional concerns of the museum quite a bit. To do this we will need to be very clear about what exactly we are up to. A museum that has been asking the question what and why in relation to its audience for some years now is the Children's Museum in Boston, USA. This museum recently put on an exhibition called 'Endings', about death. The museologists concerned thought through extremely carefully what aspects of death the exhibition should address and came up with a mixed show. There were some objects relating to funerary rituals and memorial rites, but a large part of the exhibition was put together to help children talk about their fears of death, and to uncover their misconceptions, and also to help parents find ways of discussing death with their children. The taboo subject was presented to introduce relevant and helpful vocabulary, objects and images. This was seen at the time by some people to be controversial, but when the American space shuttle blew up last spring it was to the Children's Museum that the national broadcasting companies turned to ask, 'How do we deal with this issue?'[16]. This is a poignant example of the importance of thinking through the role of a museum in the world of today, and in the light of the needs of its specific public.

Social Changes

The nature of the general public is changing in ways that museums should pay attention to. Leisure forecasters point out that the 'under-fours' as a segment of the population is growing and that young families will be increasingly evident in the profile of museum visitors[17]. Museums are already aware that family provision has become an important educational task, and family centres, workshops, activity sheets and walks have been organised. Now provision for very young families will be required. 'Grey power' is also becoming a feature to be reckoned with, not in terms of increasing numbers, but in terms of increasing spending power. Elderly people have more discretionary spending power than in the past, their health

is better, and they have a lot of free time[18]. Looking at museum audience surveys, this group is regularly conspicuous by its absence[19]. New audiences can be built by special detailed well-designed and relevant provision. Programmes for special audiences are fairly common in the United States, particularly in art galleries. There are special art classes for the very old held at Brooklyn Museum[20], and the Metropolitan Museum of Art in New York holds parent, or grandparent, and child basic art classes that sound very exciting[21]. Outreach work, both for young families and for older people is a good way to introduce these groups to the museum world, and the techniques for this kind of workshop have been developed by community workers[22]. Of course, physical facilities will be required at the museum. I never cease to be amazed at how slow we are in providing the most basic of facilities for people. As for somewhere to sort out the young families, I only know of one museum in the UK that has a decent baby changing room[23]. (It is of course, a Mother and Baby Room, but let's not get too ambitious all at once!) Museums overseas often hire out pushchairs or baby-carrying sacks and provide small scale loos and water fountains at a low level.

Other aspects of leisure characteristics should be noted. The amount of discretionary free-time is likely to increase, but overall it is more likely to be spent at home. In response to this, leisure providers, and providers of services of all sorts are moving towards the 'total destination' concept. This is the provision of a variety of services in one complex that will tempt the family out of the home, where the car can be parked, and the shopping can get done, while the children play. New museums are now often being designed as part of such a complex. Jorvik has nearby parking facilities and is part of a shopping and eating area. The vast scheme at La Villette in Paris includes a science museum, a music centre, a theatre, a pop music hall, a riding school and a large park. A new scheme in North Shropshire, now in the planning stage, involves the museum service along with other leisure services in the design of facilities for a 'short break' holiday in the area. Older museums that do not have these intrinsic advantages are beginning to find ways into busy areas, with graphic displays in parts of the shopping mall, or in the streets, or in a 'shop window' display in the underground.

The Henley Centre states that people are now tending to distinguish themselves less by their occupation or profession and more by their interests, skills or knowledge[24]. We are seeing the emergence of the discriminating consumer who wants an individualised, personalised, participative experience during her or his leisure time[25]. Detailed museum audience research from America[26], Canada[27], and Sweden[28] confirms this. People who go often to museums feel comfortable with the displays, but want to take things a bit further by having some sort of personal participation, while people who don't go often feel ill at ease and are not quite sure how to get to grips with the museum message. This latter group consistently asks for more personal help and involvement, in order to enable them to feel at ease and at home[29]. All educationalists know that true learning cannot take place unless the learner feels comfortable and in control of the situation. Infrequent museum visitors feel out of their depth and unless an effort is made on their behalf, they leave the

building in that slightly bewildered and disorientated state that is familiar to anyone arriving in a strange place and not finding any signs to help sort things out[30].

A useful feature to note in relation to museums and the leisure market is that the experience of the museum is the one that most people feel most ambivalent about. In comparison with other leisure time pursuits, the experience of the museum is undefined and vague[31]. At the same time, most people have a very positive image of the museum as a 'good thing', even if they don't often go[32]. There is a readiness in many people to be persuaded that the museum has something for them. This can be seen very clearly in some of the work recently undertaken by the museums in Leicester. During the last four years much work has been done to make the museums relevant and useful for the large proportion of the population of Leicester city that is of Asian origin. This has included collecting, putting on exhibitions, and running educational programmes for adults and children, including workshops and demonstrations[33]. The response has been enormous and lasting. A new exhibition put together for Caribbean Year looks as though it will have a similar impact. Two new appointments were made in order to develop community networks and new strategies of working and as a result Leicester is one of the few museums that can genuinely say that it has some relevance to the multi-cultural society that makes up the Britain of the late twentieth century[34].

A further aspect of social change that is of vital importance to the museum and its educational work is the development of information technology. We are already surrounded by much information of many different types. Newspapers, books, films, radio, TV, computers, advertising hoardings, signs, are continually competing for our attention. This is increasing at an exponential rate. Our skills of meaning-formation, constrained by biology and education, struggle to deal with ever increasing speeds of transmission and quantities of information. Information overload tends to lead to a reduction rather than a growth in knowledge and understanding[35].

The one thing that all this information has in common is that the messages that it conveys are pre-digested interpretations of the world. Ideas have been sifted through, turned round, mediated, for many different reasons before we, the consumer, get the message. We have little opportunity to respond. The message is one way and reality is already defined for us. The museum, because it holds real things, offers the possibility of the power to make new interpretations. Working with material objects, we can slow down the information transmission process and allow individuals to make their own sense of what they have before them. This is not to make the mistake of thinking that objects in museums are not also mediated and held in an interpretative framework. They are, and increasingly this is being examined[36]. The strength of the museum is that it, to a great extent, controls its own framework and can reinterpret objects, or offer to visitors the opportunity to make their own meanings and interpretations. This active construction of meaning is so basic and crucial to what we mean by being human, that this potential of the museum is in fact absolutely vital.

The proliferation of processed information and pre-digested interpretations brings the importance of the 'raw data' of the museum to the fore. In organising access to objects through handling sessions, museum educators can offer to visitors the possibility of taking the initiative in interpreting part of the world, and can enable people to be in control of their own processes of understanding and knowing in a way that is restorative and leads to self respect. The accuracy of the understanding is, in my view, secondary to the process of making meaning itself. It doesn't really matter if, in trying to understand a new object, the accepted curatorial interpretation is not the interpretation that is arrived at. There are many ways to make sense of the world and its things, and interpretations vary throughout both social and individual time. It is more important to enable people to take understanding into their own hands and to develop through practice the skills of observation, comparison and deduction.

Educational Changes

Changes in the structure and content of the secondary school exam system both in England and Scotland are shifting the emphases of attention from abstract to concrete experiences. The criteria for the examination syllabi for the Scottish Standard Grade, and the English GCSE and CPVE, all emphasise the process of knowing rather than the accumulation of knowledge. Skills that enable learning and investigative studies are more important than the reiteration of facts. A quote from the Guide to the Scottish Standard Grade Exams spells this out; 'There will be a move away from simply learning facts about a subject towards learning skills and understanding ideas. In Science, for example, learning how to handle information and how to tackle investigations will be stressed'. The National Criteria for GCSE History states that students should be able 'to locate and extract information from primary and secondary sources', and 'to understand the nature and use of historical evidence'. There is a demand from all sides to produce courses that enable children to get to grips in a practical way with real things, in real places. Instead of individualistic learning with children in rows in front of the teacher, this approach encourages site visits, group learning, and concrete experiences that enable children to discuss in groups and to work together, making sense of reality as they experience it. This has been commonplace in some primary schools and in the classrooms of some of the less able older students for many years. It has also been found in some art or drama classes in secondary schools. In many other areas it is regarded as a new and radical approach. However, for the last hundred years this way of working has been quietly developing in the museum.

Learning from real things and real places, talking, handling, discussing, reviewing, comparing, recording and presenting, all these methods are used every day by museum teachers. Consequently, there is a reservoir of experience in museum education that could now be of great use to the educational world in general. Teachers are being asked to teach from material things. Very few teacher-training courses, until very recently, included this as part of their syllabus. Techniques of using material things to teach from have been developed in museums for a very long time and are well tried[37]. Teachers are being asked to organise visits and to enable learning outside the classroom. This too is often neglected as a part of some teacher-training courses. Many visits are planned with little awareness of how and what learning may be possible, and how learning can be either facilitated or prevented by the practical organisation of the day. Again, experienced museum teachers see good and bad practice every day and know which criteria apply.

The new exam syllabi emphasise a cross-curricular approach, and an effort to relate learning experiences to the everyday life experiences of the child. This is something that has not been a common aspect of many classrooms, but is unavoidable in educational work in a museum. Working with real things, it is soon clear how arbitrary are our existing subject boundaries. A painting can make sense as part of an art lesson, looking at the use of paint and the subject matter, but it may also reveal much historical information, can be a good motivator for writing, and talking, could fit into a social studies programme, could relate to an urban studies programme and so on. Relationships between objects can be made to reveal contrasts, and developments; to lead to further questioning; to inspire a need to know that guides the learner to research material, and then back to the object.

One of the strengths of using material things in teaching is that the same things can be relevant at many different levels of knowing. Museum teachers are used to teaching the same artefact to both beginning and experienced learners, at all points on the scale of specialised knowledge acquisition, and at all age levels. With this experience, museum teachers become skilled in predicting the specific aspect of an artefact, or a group of artefacts, that will suit the needs of particular learners. At the same time, a reservoir of knowledge of other aspects of the object enables a response to wide-ranging questions from the learners.

Interpreter at work at Quarry Bank Mill, Styal.

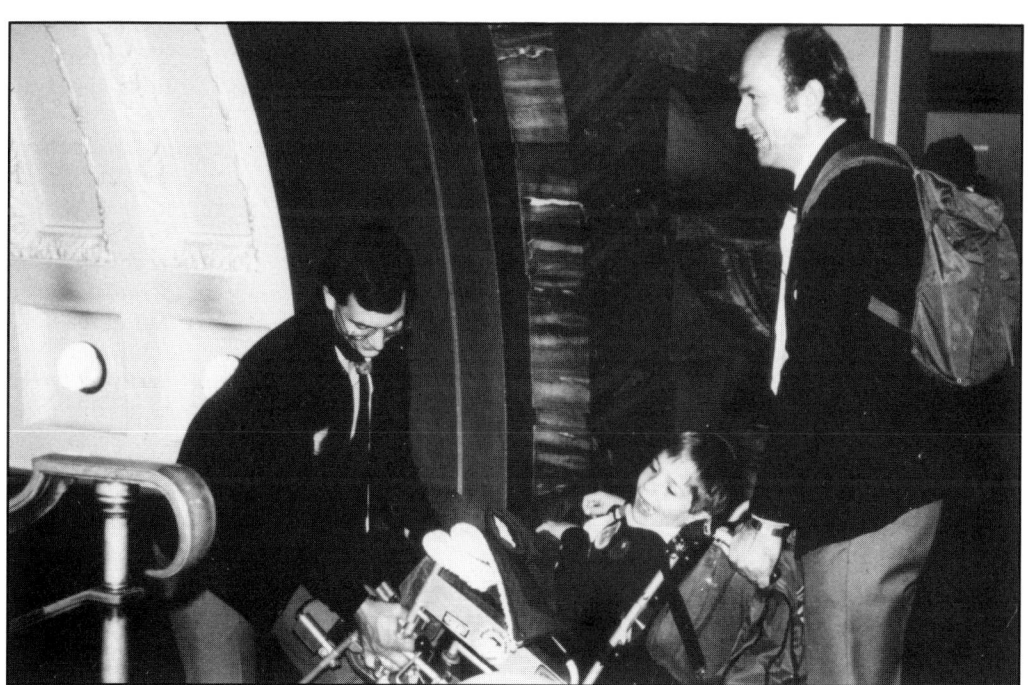

Nineteenth-century museum buildings cause problems for wheelchair access.

Objects not only open the way from one subject area to another, they require the use of various skills in order to decipher them. Students are able to develop skills of close observation, of questioning, of discussion, of talking, of documentation, of comparison, of making links and connections. And in their discussions and observations, students inevitably draw on what they already know, and build bridges between this and the new things they are looking at. This happens at an almost unconscious level, in the struggle to find a meaning for the object under review. Helpful and discreet questions to enable further looking and accurate deductions allow the museum educator to act as a facilitator in the learning process rather than a transmitter of their own knowledge. Learning in the museum is process- rather than product-oriented. Museum educationalists know all too well that handing over a tight package of facts is the fastest way of alienating all but the most motivated audience, and have developed skills of collaborative discovery to use instead.

An important aspect of real things in the learning process is their use as a motivator. Even with my students at post-graduate level, there is an extremely marked difference in response when I ask them to work with objects from the museum loan service, rather than listen to me or talk to each other. Research has shown that the same things can be learnt either with or without objects, but that the ideas that were learnt with the real objects to help were absorbed more easily and with greater enthusiasm, were remembered longer, and generated an enthusiasm to know more[38]. We know that the acquisition of information does not equal understanding. True internalised understanding that is genuinely felt and incorporated into the existing knowledge and experience of the learner is more likely to occur in concrete situations.

At this time when teachers are likely to be looking for guidance as to how to develop their teaching skills to work in new ways, I feel that museum education has much to offer. Teachers may not know this, of course, and it may well be up to the museum to step forward and to offer to become involved. But I think that now, there is an opportunity to put museum education on the educational map in a way that has not happened before, and in a way that will inevitably lead to a greater emphasis on the educational aspects of museum work. We have seen how the future of museums lies with the services that it provides for the public. It is clear that a museum in future will be measured by its ability to care for people, and I suggest that the time is now ripe for museum educators to step forward.

Museum Education; the way forward
What does all this actually mean in practice? Let's look at the broad implications first. It means that museums must begin to consider the use rather than the increase of collections as a primary factor, and that a genuine educational and social emphasis should be part of the day to day concerns of all museum workers. It means that the museum should develop clear policies and both long and short term objectives in relation to their visitors[39]. This should be done on a basis of research[40]. This means more than just measuring who comes to the museum. The existing and the potential visitor profiles need to be related[41].

We have seen that new groups are likely to influence the leisure market in general, those of young families and older adults. Particular attention should be paid to broad provision for these people, including basic physical provision, and the development of outreach work. The nature of the work with the immigrant communities in both Leicester and Bradford has demonstrated the importance of local networks, and of the museum worker working alongside existing community groups, and these methods could be used for other groups too. Where the museum serves a community that may have conflicting elements within it, some experience indicates that the museum may be seen as neutral territory, and it may therefore be in a position to enable cultural cross-fertilisation[42].

I have not said much about the displays in the museum, and some may think that this is outside the purview of museum education as such. However, I think we should not put talks and workshops into one compartment and displays into another. The entire public face of the museum will inevitably have an educational function. However, many displays are difficult for many people. Very many displays relate to a highly specialised academic knowledge area. These are often difficult to grasp. Theme-based exhibitions, or exhibitions designed around everyday subject matter is more accessible, and not impossible to do. Last year the Museum of Popular Arts and Traditions in Paris put on an exhibition called 'La France et la Table', which was able to show collections of both artefacts and images, but also allow people to make relationships with their everyday experiences. On the basis of comparison with well-known activities, the museum's collections take on more relevance and

therefore become more able to be appreciated. The Livesey Museum in South London recently got together a show to enable people to recall local birth, death and marriage customs. The aim of the exhibition was to stimulate conversation about particular events. In some cases with exhibitions such as these, sections of the community are involved in bringing objects to the museum, and people are able to make their own contribution[43]. This is a very different thing from putting on show the objects in the collection because they happen to be around.

Labels are very often not that helpful[44]. At the Children's Museum, in Boston, labels are written on three levels: one for the adult with a little knowledge, one for the child, and one for the parent to read out to the child. This acknowledges that most of us are beginning learners at almost everything. It also recognises a most important point, that we learn through our children. The labels that can be read to the child enable the parent to have some answer to the questions, and to absorb some new information in an unobtrusive and painless way[45].

Part of the educational role of the museum consists in enabling people to understand the tasks and processes that make up the work of the museum. This is generally very little known about, and yet people find it fascinating. It is often the case that the unknown appears incomprehensible and therefore meaningless. If we can offer to people the possibility of learning about museum concerns through involvement then we may do much to increase public sympathy for the museum. For example, a recent project at the Museum of Mankind in

London, linked to the exhibition 'Lost Magic Kingdoms', enabled both adults and children to discover the criteria for the exhibition and to develop their own criteria and their own exhibition through practical activity. A Swedish project that started out as an adult education art class led to the participants designing their own art exhibition. They were involved in the process of the museum, and therefore began to relate to it in a way that would not have been possible without this personal participation and commitment[46].

We could learn another trick from the States, and that is the use of interpreters. This is an interesting feature of some American museums, including Boston[47]. At Boston, young people are used to walk the floors and to talk to visitors. They are generally doing this as part of a high school project, or they are older students doing a longer term of attachment as work experience. Extensive training and support programmes are organised for them, and they work with visitors at a number of different levels. These vary from talking and discussing exhibits, to being part of an exhibit, to running activities or demonstrations in relation to exhibits. This has been worked out in extraordinary detail and is most professionally organised. The new gallery at the Science Museum, 'Launch Pad', is working on these principles. In short, displays can be made more accessible in many ways and museum educationalists are increasingly being asked by their curatorial colleagues to contribute in this area.

Two recent surveys have looked at the relationship of schools to museums, though in rather different ways. 'The Market for Educational Visits to Tourist Attractions'[48]

takes a marketing approach to school visits to museums, theme-parks, zoos, theatres and historic buildings. It points out that there were over 11 million educational visits to attractions in England in 1984, a market worth £7.5 million in admissions alone. The most popular types of attraction were historic buildings, theatres and museums and art galleries. In discussing the provision for the visit by the attraction, the report states that 83% of attractions made special provision for educational visits, but that fewer museums did so than other types of attraction. Thus only 77% of museums provided special facilities, when 100% of zoos did, and 84% of historic houses did[49]. Provisions included picnic areas, teachers' packs, audio-visual facilities, specialist staff, and lecture rooms. It went on to say that where special provision had been made the visits were twice as long, and also that out of all the special things provided what teachers really wanted most were the teachers' packs to help them plan their visit well. It would appear from this that in relation to other types of attraction, the museum is popular, but that because there is less special provision, the visit is more difficult to organise, harder work, and therefore the visits are shorter and possibly less productive.

The second report, although it has a very different approach, also points out that teachers do not always organise their visits well and that they need help with this. This is the DES report *A Survey of the Use Some Hertfordshire Schools Make of Museum Services*[50]. This, as might be expected, is much more concerned for the educational viability of the use of museums, and points to good practice and also to some problems. The report identifies a lack on the part of teachers of clear and demanding criteria on which to base both the museum visit and the follow-up work in school. It also says that teachers would like a preliminary pack with a bibliography, work suggestions and illustrations. The report emphasises the need for in-service training to help teachers make better use of museums by developing their organisational and teaching skills.

It would seem from both of these reports that much more work with groups of teachers is required. We need to run in-service training programmes for them to develop their skills, but we also need to work together to develop more in-depth work programmes. The report praises a project that stretched across several museums and many subject areas, and involved many different ways of working, using the expertise of different adults. In-depth and long term projects such as these, if they are carefully planned and then documented, would do much to make museum education methods more generally available and to

improve practice generally. The development of teaching materials that could be used to illustrate museum methods would be of great use to teacher trainers[51]. It is also clear that introductory pre-visit material is required for many museum visitors including teachers, children and families. Some of the National Museums in London are showing the way here, particularly the British Museum and the Science Museum. Sponsorship is sometimes available for some educational activities, and should be considered.

In conclusion, I think the way is clear for museum education in the next twenty years. The museum must swing its emphasis away from collections and towards people, with the aim of maximising its resources, and in the worlds both of the general public and of education there are clearly identifiable targets for this swing to encompass. It is time for the museum educator to step forward with greater confidence than ever before.

Sources

I should like to thank John Reeve, Education Service, British Museum, for his helpful and speedy comments after having read the first draft of this paper.

1.   C. Cooper and J. Latham, *The Market for Educational Visits to Tourist Attractions,* Department of Tourism and Field Sciences, Dorset Institute of Higher Education, 1985.
2.   See for example many of the papers from the symposium, *Making Exhibitions of Ourselves: the Limits of Objectivity in the Representation of Other Cultures,* Association of Social Anthropologists and Museum Ethnographers' Group, British Museum, London, February 13th-15th, 1986.
3.   A group was established in 1983 to examine the issues of women's history and women's practice in museums. The first conference papers review the main issues. *Wham! Women, Heritage and Museums,* Social History Curator's Group, Woolton Hall, Fallowfield, Manchester, April 7th-8th, 1984.
4.   J. Peirson-Jones 'Responding to a Multi-Cultural Society: Which Africa? Which Arts?' *Museum Ethnographers' Group Newsletter,* 19, 1985, pp. 15-25.
5.   R. Attenborough, *Arts and Disabled People,* and A. Pearson, *Arts for Everyone,* 1985, both published by Carnegie UK and CEH.
6.   See for example E. Hooper-Greenhill, *The National Portrait Gallery – A Case-Study in Cultural Reproduction,* MA dissertation, 1980, Department of

Sociology of Education, University of London and D. J. Meltzer, 'Ideology and Material Culture', in R. A. Gould & M. B. Schiffer, (eds), *Modern Material Culture: The Archaeology of Us,* Academic Press, 1981, pp. 113-25.

7.   J. Mackenzie, 'Representations of the Hunter in the Late 19th and 20th Centuries'. Paper delivered at the *Representations* symposium, British Museum, 1986.

8.   D. Horne, *The Great Museum,* London and Sydney, 1984.

9.   P. Wright, *On Living in an Old Country,* London, 1985.

10.   See for example T. J. Schlereth 'Contemporary collecting for future recollecting', *Museum Studies Journal,* VI(3), 1984; John F. Kennedy University, San Francisco and 'Twentieth Century Recording', *Museums Journal,* 85(1), 1985.

11.   E. Hooper-Greenhill, *Power/Knowledge in the Museum (provisional title),* PhD dissertation, Department of Sociology of Education, University of London, 1987.

12.   R. Strong 'The museum game', *The Listener,* 25th July, 1985, pp. 17-19.

13.   See for example, N. Cossons, 'The museums boom: when is a museum not a museum?' *The Listener,* 2nd August, 1984, pp. 13-17.

14.   Detailed research on perceptions of this exhibition has been carried out by Maria Barretto as part of her PhD dissertation on *Museum Semiotics,* Department of Museum Studies, University of Leicester.

15.   M. A. Munley, 'Monitoring trends in museums', *Museum News,* 63(5), 1985, pp. 69-77.

16.   This was pointed out to me by Stephen Feber, Director of the Children's Museum's Eureka! project.

17.   The Henley Centre for Forecasting, *Leisure Futures,* London, 1986.

18.   ibid, pp. 43-44.

19.   For a comprehensive bibliography of museum visitor surveys, see *A Bibliography for Museum Studies Training,* Department of Museum Studies, University of Leicester, 1986.

20.   I. Heffernan and S. Schnee 'Building a new museum audience', *Museum News,* 59(5), 1981, pp. 31-32. See also L. Graetz, 'Houston: a steady hand and a peaceful heart', *Museum News,* 59(5), 1981, pp. 33-35.

21.   E. Hooper-Greenhill, 'Museum and Education', report prepared for the UNESCO conference on *Museum and Education,* Guadalajara, Mexico, March 1986, p. 8. This report consists of a review and summary of 69 articles collected for UNESCO by ICOM/CECA. Both the original articles and the report are available for consultation at the Department of Museum Studies, University of Leicester.

22.   G. Mertz, *An object in the hand . . . Museum Educational Outreach for the Elderly, Incarcerated & Disabled,* Smithsonian Institution Collaborative Educational Outreach Program, 1981. This is an exemplary account of the problems and potentials of museum outreach work with 'immobile populations'.

23.   At the National Railway Museum, York.

24.   The Henley Centre for Forecasting, op. cit. (note 17), p. 14.

25.   Cossons makes this point in relation to museums; op. cit. (note 13), p. 17.

26.   M. G. Hood, 'Staying away – why people choose not to visit museums', *Museum News,* 6(14), 1983, pp. 50-57.

27.   B. Dixon et al., *The Museum and the Canadian Public, Arts and Culture Branch,* Department of the Secretary of State, Toronto, 1974.

28.   V. Arnell et al., *Going to exhibitions,* Riksutställningar/Swedish travelling exhibitions, Stockholm, 1976.

29.   P. Bourdieu, *L'amour de l'art: les musees d'art européens et leur public,* Editions de Minuit, Paris, 1969; P. Bourdieu, 'Class and Culture: the work of Bourdieu', *Media, Culture and Society,* 2, (3), 1980; E. Hooper-Greenhill, 'Art gallery audiences and class constraints', *Bullet,* 5-8, 24th January, 1985.

30.   P. Mann, *Visitors to the British Museum, four surveys,* Lectures (taped in 1984 and 1985) to the Department of Museum Studies, University of Leicester. See Marjorie Caygill and Geoffrey House (eds.), *A Survey of visitors to the British Museum* (1982-1983), British Museum, London, 1986 for the published version of this work.

31.   B. Dixon, op. cit. (note 27), pp. 44-45.

32.   ibid, pp. 128-29. See also D. Prince and R. T. Schadla-Hall, 'The image of the museum: a case-study of Kingston-upon-Hull', *Museums Journal,* 85(91), pp. 39-45.

33.   J. Nicholson, 'The museum and the Indian community; findings and orientation of the Leicestershire Museums Service', *Museum*

Ethnographers' Group Newsletter, 19, 1985, pp. 3-14.

34.   There is a great interest in multi-cultural work in museums at the moment and many meetings are being held to discuss how work should proceed. New appointments have also been made recently in Ipswich, Bradford, and Kirklees. For the training implications see E. Hooper-Greenhill, 'Training for change: museum work in the multi-cultural society', paper prepared for the seminar *Museums' responses to the multi-cultural society,* Cartwright Hall, Bradford, 6th June, 1986. This was organised by WHAM! (Yorkshire) and it is hoped that the papers will be published shortly.

35.   G. O'Neill, 'Blip-Culture', in The Henley Centre for Forecasting, op. cit. (note 17), pp. 18-22.

36.   Many of the contributions to the British Museum *Representations* symposium, op. cit. (note 2), tackled exactly this topic. See for example, J. Reeve 'Leading the public to Nirvana? Interpreting Buddhism: Art and Faith'.

37.   For a comprehensive museum education bibliography see *Learning Goals and Bibliography for Museum Studies Training; Museum Education Services Option* (50 pages, updated annually). For a general statement on the nature of museum education see in particular E. Hooper-Greenhill, 'Some basic principles and issues relating to museum education', *Museums Journal,* 82(2/3), 1983, pp. 120-30. Two of the best articles on teaching with objects are C. Adams and S. Miller, 'Museums and the use of evidence in history teaching', *Teaching History,* 34, 1982, and Hennigar-Shuh, 'Teaching yourself to teach with objects', *Journal of Education,* Nova Scotia, 7, (4), 1982.

38.   M. Borun and B. K. Flexer, *The impact of a class visit to a science museum – an experimental study,* The Franklin Institute Science Museum, USA, n.d.

39.   A professional attitude to visitor services underlies much of the report published by the British Tourist Authority, *Museums – lessons from the USA,* 1983, which was compiled after a visit to America by a group of leading museum professionals.

40.   Museum visitor surveys are generally small-scale and often suffer from amateurism. A good review of some of the main problems is contained in R. J. Loomis, 'Please not another visitor survey', *Museum News,* 52(2), 1973, pp. 21-26. Professional surveys include B. Dixon, op. cit. (note 27), and P. Mann, op. cit. (note 30).

41.   Surveys of this nature have been organised by the Tyne and Wear Museums Service.

42.   This is said to be the case at the Children's Museum, Boston, which is sited in dockland at the interstices of four different inner-city ethnic areas.

43.   H. De Varine-Bohan, 'A "fragmented" museum – the Museum of Man and Industry, Le Creuseau-Montceau-les-Mines', *Museum,* 25(4), 1973, pp. 242-49.

44.   B. D. Sorsby and S. D. Horne, 'The readability of museum labels', *Museums Journal,* 80(3), 1980, pp. 157-59. These authors point out that three-quarters of visitors to museums have difficulty with two-thirds of the labels because of their vocabulary and difficult sentence structure.

45.   E. H. Gurian, *The Children's Museum, Boston and its interpretive policy,* lecture in the Department of Museum Studies, University of Leicester, 1985.

46.   U. Arnell, op. cit. (note 28), pp. 118-21.

47.   See also British Tourist Authority, op. cit. (note 39), p. 10.

48.   E. Cooper and J. Latham, op. cit. (note 1).

49.   ibid. pp. 14-16. The sample of attractions was chosen to obtain a balance of geographical location, size and type of attraction. 44 museum and art galleries were used. No details as to the type of governing body of these institutions is given in the report.

50.   Department of Education and Science, *A survey of the use some Hertfordshire schools make of museum services,* London, 1986.

51.   A Local Authority Adviser from Bradford will be based in the Department of Museum Studies, University of Leicester, on a year's Teacher Fellowship from September, 1986. As part of his research into resource-based learning, he will be producing and collating teaching materials of this nature.

Mary Queen of Scots Celebration Day at the Scottish National Portrait Gallery.

Today's Dustbins, Tomorrow's Museums: Developments in Museum Education in Scotland

Mary Bryden

Mary Bryden is Head of Education in the National Museums of Scotland. In 1979 after an early career in secondary teaching she joined the National Museum of Antiquities of Scotland as Education and Public Relations Officer. She has been actively engaged in developing the new education service of the National Museums of Scotland since 1985.

Introduction

I have been asked to survey developments in museum education in Scotland.[1] To some extent this has been done already. Since the time of writing this the Miles Report has been published[2]. The Scottish Museums Council has, in association with the Glasgow Herald, published a clear, concise and well-illustrated guide to Scottish Museums and Galleries[3]. It is full of stirring thoughts:

'Scotland's museums and galleries are among the finest in the world. The 400 institutions featured in this guide present the visitor with an unrivalled richness and variety of experiences . . . some 12 million visits will be made to Scotland's museums and galleries this year, reflecting the enthusiasm of Scots and tourists alike for what they have to offer. For museums are more popular now than at any time in their 300 year history – they have become a real medium of mass communication.'

Thus writes Graeme Farnell, formerly Director of the Scottish Museums Council. But hold on – is the picture as rosy as that as far as museum education is concerned? An article by Stewart Coulter, Education Officer, Glasgow Art Gallery and Museums, suggests that it is not:

'In Scotland only a handful of museums have official education departments with specialist staff – Aberdeen, Dundee, Edinburgh, Glasgow, Hamilton, Paisley and Perth.'

Only a handful – out of 400? It's not very impressive is it? Let's check this one out. Back to the Council's guide. I searched through it looking for references to children, young people, workshops and education, educational activities, and teaching material: anything that might suggest an education officer in post, or a curator concerned about education.

Bowhill: 'School packs, teachers' guide.'

Bo'ness & Kinneil Railway: 'Special school fortnights every year.'

Drumlanrig Castle: 'Pre-booked school parties welcome for nature trail and castle projects.'

Kirkcaldy: 'School services available.'

Dunnet Bay Pavilion: 'Children are encouraged to bring in their own shells and objects for identification and to look at their finer details using a simple microscope.'

Myreton Motor Museum, Aberfeldy: 'A Museum quiz book is available for children.'

Cockburn Museum, Department of Geology, Edinburgh University: '. . . teaching material available.'

National Gallery, Edinburgh: 'The education department for the National Galleries provides workshops, projects etc for schools.'

Royal Museum of Scotland: 'The education department provides an active programme for children and adults including lectures, concerts, films, competitions, workshops and other related activities.'

Royal Observatory Visitor Centre, Edinburgh: 'An excellent educational facility, the centre provides lectures, films, talks and projects for schools and societies.'

369 Gallery, Edinburgh: 'Schools' education room holds lectures, classes, workshops. Afternoon and evening classes and special projects for unemployed are held regularly.'

Pier Arts Centre, Stromness: 'A special feature of the gallery is the Children's Room where young visitors can produce and display their own work.'

Isle of Arran Heritage Museum: 'Arran High School Heritage Projects are also exhibited here.'

Gladstone Court Museum, Biggar: 'School worksheets available.'

Greenhill Covenanters' House: 'School worksheets available.'

Summerlee Heritage Park, Coatbridge: 'Educational activities will be provided on site.'

Baird Institute Museum, Cumnock: 'Worksheets are available for children.'

Cathcartston Interpretation Centre, Dalmellington: 'Facilities can be provided for school pupils and students.'

Art Gallery and Museum, Kelvingrove, Glasgow: 'Competitions for children during school holidays, daily guided tours, regular events organised. Contact the education department for details of lessons for school parties, the annual schoolchildren's art competition and other activities.'

Barony Chambers Museum, Kirkintilloch: 'Classes, special activities and worksheets can be provided for schools and museum staff are available for school visits.'

Hagg's Castle, Glasgow: 'Crafts workshops for children are held regularly.'

Hamilton District Museum: 'The education officer provides a wide range of services for school parties and other groups.'

Rutherglen Museum: 'A schoolchildren's art competition is held annually.'

Dundee Printmakers' Workshop: 'Educational facilities are available.'

McManus Galleries, Dundee: 'For information on the active schools programme which includes lectures, visits, workshops, school loan service, publications, holiday activities, contact the extension services department.'

But what does all this mean? Rather than take you on a Cook's tour of all of these I am going to concentrate on specific examples which show good traditional museum education, or which show interesting new developments, or which show good use of Manpower Services Commission schemes, or which show excellent working relationships between curator and education officer, or which show imaginative curators attracting young people into their museums.

Symbols of Power at the time of Stonehenge: an education programme

Leaving aside Glasgow Art Gallery and Museums and the National Trust for Scotland, which you will read about later, I am going to start off quite unashamedly with an education programme at the National Museums of Scotland.

In the summer of 1985 in the then National Museum of Antiquities of Scotland we put on an exhibition called *Symbols of Power at the time of Stonehenge*[4].

Talk to any non-specialist and it quickly becomes clear that the widespread view of prehistoric peoples is of squat, grunting savages, whose existence was a round of unremitting toil: prehistory seems so difficult to understand that it is hardly surprising that some have tried to explain prehistoric monuments in terms of extra-terrestrial visitors: at least initially it seems very difficult for many people to relate to the very distant past. Even a visit to a prehistoric monument or a look at some of the objects does not necessarily shake a very fundamental picture of the people who built the monuments and produced the objects; it is perhaps easier to retain these rather vague, bland images. As a result the public, academic and non-academic alike, are accustomed to the sort of exhibitions such as those on the Vikings held a few years ago in London, New York and Stockholm – good examples of how it is thought appropriate or safer when looking at archaeology to review a broad range of activities in a way that museum curators would never dream of considering for more recent periods. Our exhibition did not do this: rather it concentrated on aspects of one particular theme, the expression of power and status, and persuaded us that prehistoric people were in fact extremely sophisticated, with aims and aspirations not unlike ours today. And that was the key into prehistory in this exhibition.

Power is something with which we are all familiar. At its most simple we are so used to it that we take it for granted when we see it every day in the form of policemen directing traffic or traffic wardens sticking tickets on illegally parked cars. However in this exhibition what we were concerned with was the use of items of material culture as symbols of power where this provided information about how people developed, held onto and finally lost power. In the 1980s being the owner of an expensive car, a piece of jewellery or a Jean Muir dress enhances status and indeed much advertising depends on presenting an object or possession in such a way that buying it will apparently underline this status. The clothes we buy and choose to wear on different occasions say a great deal about our social position and values. Badges, ties and scarves show what we belong to, be it something as obvious as membership of a football club or something much less definable like showing apparent good taste by wearing a Hermes scarf. While in prehistoric societies choice in our eyes would have seemed very restrictive, nevertheless what might have been as important then could have been the acquisition of knowledge or a certain skill: not much has changed!

Another obvious symbol of power in the 20th century is that of a uniform. While it is often argued that there are perfectly practical reasons for uniforms, it is also clear that a uniform means association with or belonging to a certain group. And what is more, there are all sorts of subtle changes and additions to uniforms to denote hierarchy: it would be difficult to confuse a Chief Constable with a bobby on the beat. And again these differences become exaggerated at ceremonial occasions, with official chains of office, maces and even crowns. Prehistoric people were no different and many objects on display in this exhibition were used in similar ways. Monuments and buildings are also symbols. Many 19th-century commercial buildings could not fail to impress their customers with their importance and solidity. And who does not buy a house or flat which says something about their status?

The themes in the exhibition, power, prestige and status, were as much a part of life in prehistory as they are today so you can begin to see our approach. What we were trying to say was that in many respects the 20th century has a great deal to learn from prehistoric times. We were trying to introduce people to prehistory by taking them in through the 20th century, through symbols of power in the 20th century that they are used to seeing, and we hoped that by the time they had gone through the exhibition they would in fact come out and look at the 20th century with new eyes.

It was important that with an exhibition like this, which brought together so much material that hadn't been together in several hundred years, and looked at the material in such a different and, we thought, exciting way, we should provide an equally exciting and demanding education programme. What could we provide? The exhibition followed an approach which was new and different: we were not saying everything that could be said about those living at the time looked at: we were not presenting the approach of 'a day in the life of Bronze Age man'; we were not presenting information about what Bronze Age people wore, or ate, or did during a normal day. Rather, we were looking at one particular area, the expression of power, and in a way we were looking, inevitably, with 20th-century eyes and trying to explain the material that had been excavated. That gave us the clue as far as the education programme was concerned: what we should do was encourage children to look at the evidence archaeologists had to work with, and see if they could put themselves in the shoes of the archaeologists. After much discussion with museum staff and a member of staff from Moray House College of Education in Edinburgh, we began to draft the information that went out to schools on the ideas behind the exhibition and the approach of the education programme including a glossary of terms used in the exhibition.

Let me take you through the different stages that the children experienced on their visit.

On arrival, the group was divided into two and each sub-group was given a dustbin – a 20th-century dustbin – to have a look at. We quite deliberately started off the session with these dustbins, because we wanted to look at what we can make of rubbish thrown away in the 1980s and what it tells you about the people who threw that rubbish away. We put together two dustbins, two contrasting dustbins, made up of rubbish from a Barnton- or Kelvinside-type dustbin and a less well-to-do type dustbin. Inevitably we exaggerated in what we chose, but we wanted to make the point fairly obvious. In our Barnton-type dustbin, which was a good quality heavy metal dustbin, we included a copy of Debrett's Peerage, an invitation to a Royal Garden Party, a bottle that had some expensive smelling scent left in it, an empty tin of olive oil from Italy, a pair of long white gloves – I am sure you get the picture. Gradually the children got the idea that this household was well-to-do, and that there didn't seem to be any children living there. The other dustbin was made of heavy plastic, and it had a blue Edinburgh District Council bag inside it which had burst. In the dustbin itself were a copy of the Beano, an empty tin of baked beans, an empty coke bottle, a book and a toy, a copy of the Daily Record, some empty crisp packets, an old tube of Smarties, a record sleeve, a copy of Woman's Own, and of course the children picked up that at the very least the family

that had thrown away this rubbish was more like them and that there were children living there. It was the sort of rubbish we would all throw out.

From there the class had to be divided into two: one group visited the exhibition looking at six key objects on display. The other group stayed in the Education Room for activities. Our activities were worked out to try to encourage the concepts of explanation as well as discovery. We gave each child a box which belonged to him or her for the session: in that box were a polythene bag with broken pieces of 1980s pottery, some plasticine, a sharp pointed piece of wood, string, shells, and a small wooden box with the label 'Fragile' containing a real archaeological object.

As you can see we wanted to present the children with several examples of evidence but most important we wanted them to use two things: imagination and their eyes. The idea of the polythene bag and its contents was to keep with the 20th-century concept and start thinking about what archaeologists do with broken pieces of pottery, or indeed a single piece of pottery, since mostly all they find is one single sherd. And the children's reaction was fascinating: some opened up their bags and set to piece together the broken pieces of plates, saucers, and soup bowls. Others took one look at the bag and its contents and said with a certain amount of disdain that it was obviously a saucer, or whatever. But with help and suggestions from us they began to look with more care and what had seemed to be too familiar and therefore not worthy of a second look, what was described quickly and inaccurately as a plate, was then seen to be a saucer by the shape of the piece in the middle; even although it did not actually say where it was made a soup plate might at least have the name of the pattern in English, so we could deduce from that that it was made in one of the English-speaking countries. The children began to realise that close examination even of very familiar objects could be rewarding.

Something every child had was a large lump of plasticine, along with the material prehistoric man had available to him to decorate his clay pots. The children were encouraged to mould pots with the plasticine and experiment with decoration. Many interesting shapes were produced and some exciting patterns, using amazing combinations of string, shells, bones and thumbnails.

However the pièce de resistance was the small box each child had, with the label 'Fragile'. In each box was a genuine archaeological object, or if it was too large to go in the box, a piece of paper telling them to report to a member of museum staff to collect their object. Objects included the following:
a selection of flint arrowheads, a ground and polished stone axe head, a stone axe hammer, a bronze flat axe head, a bronze sword, some pieces of Bronze Age pottery, a stone hammer, bone pins, a spindle whorl, and a human jaw bone.

Each child had to imagine that he or she had just excavated that object and had to work out what it was. There were certain questions they could ask themselves. What was it made of? How common was that raw material? How easy was it to obtain? How was it made? How easy was it to make? Did it require special skills or special equipment to make it? If so, what did that tell us about the people who made it? Who might have used it? Where was it used? How old was the object? Why did some materials survive and others not? How did we know? We had originally planned that each child would fill in an archaeological record form. As we tried to draft it, we got more and more bogged down: then we thought about using a computer and we programmed the computer to ask the child very simple questions about the object. If the child was having difficulty, the computer put up various possible answers and eventually everyone got a print-out with his or her assessment of the object which he or she could then compare with the print-out showing the Museum's assessment of the object.

The children's ideas about the objects were imaginative, yet based on the evidence available. A bone pin was surprising: it was polished; they could try it out as a hair decoration or a pin for their jersey; they noticed the different colours; they were fascinated that something as ordinary as a bone could be shaped and polished into something both ornamental and functional. The human jaw, complete with teeth, needless to say was very popular: they were surprised at the smoothness of the teeth which led to a discussion of what people ate in those days. What seemed to matter was that everyone had their own box, with their own object and therefore felt valued and trusted as an individual. In letters from the children the words most often used to describe their day at the Museum were 'exciting', 'fun', and 'brilliant'. One particular school did some marvellous follow-up work: indeed many schools did some quite fascinating art work but one primary school put on an entire exhibition in their classroom called 'Symbols of Power'. They had made pots, using self-drying clay, which were the correct shape for prehistoric pots, with wonderful patterns; they had copied some of the mysterious carved stone balls; they had collected useful pebbles and flint from a visit to the seashore from which they made loom weights; they made a mini-Stonehenge in a sand tray; with a role of gold foil they made lunulae and gold capes with decoration pressed out from the back – exactly similar to the method used for the Bronze Age lunulae and cape; they had also written a play and story specially for the exhibition.

This whole programme was for us one of the most rewarding we had ever laid on: we certainly learnt a great deal from it and we are assured that our clientele were delighted.

More education programmes in Scottish Museums and Galleries

But that was an example in a National Museum with resources, funding and staffing. What other examples should we look at?

Take the David Livingstone Centre, Blantyre, run by a private trust. An Education Officer was appointed in 1984: she has a teaching background and sees her job as developing the social history side of the Centre as well as working with groups of all ages when they visit, and indeed going out to schools to talk about the collections. Here you find a good example of sound Museum education: she has attracted all the head teachers in Lanark to an in-service day; she expects and gets a great deal out of a visiting group; she encourages drama and role play; she insists every child wriggles through a small and unpleasant tunnel she has created in the part of the museum leading to the section on

mining and, with a vivid mixture of objects and photographs, models and imagination, maps and figures she brings to life what it was like working in Blantyre in David Livingstone's time. This is a good contrast to the experiences the group has already had going round the tenement he grew up in and looking at the exhibition on his experiences in Africa.

An interesting development in several museums with Education Officers is the renaming of their post so that they are now called Extension Officers or are part of Extension Services. An Education post in a museum is less likely now to mean Schools Officer but rather someone concerned with education in the broadest sense – communication – and with education as a lifelong process. The Keeper of Extension Services in Aberdeen for example sees it as part of his remit to push out the museum walls: to provide films, videos, dance and drama for all ages, to put on workshops for children and adults, to organise recitals, lectures, talks, readings, artists in residence – in other words to offer opportunities for the public to enjoy the Arts in the widest possible sense, since he firmly believes that if they enjoy an experience they learn almost without realising it. He has a good budget for visiting artists and experts: some events are free, others have a charge.

Time and time again my colleagues in museum education throughout Scotland stress the importance of good relations with curatorial staff within the museum on the one hand and with advisers in the local education authority and staff at colleges of education on the other. Cooperation, liaison, call it what you want, is *vital* in making museum education work. As long as museum education staff are given displays to interpret only when curatorial staff have already put them up, their talents are being wasted. Of course museums must collect, conserve and research but they must also communicate. While the research element gives depth to what museums are trying to do, the communication element gives breadth: both these elements are vital for the success of any museum. The first essential then in education is to ensure that displays are visually stimulating in a way that engages the public's attention, which inspires the visitor, which makes him or her more curious – it is up to all of us, curatorial and education staff alike, to make sure the public enjoy their museum experience and get a lot of satisfaction out of it.

An interesting example of the kind of co-operation I mean can be seen in Dundee where the Head of Extension Services and one of his department, a seconded teacher, have been very heavily involved in the exciting new galleries in the Museum there. In 1980 the City of Dundee District Council gave a major financial commitment for the refurbishment of the then Albert Institute: new educational facilities, a lecture room and a classroom/activities area were developed. The museum has been renamed the McManus Galleries and a programme of interpretative displays concentrating on human history is being developed. The gallery on Trade and Industry, on this occasion co-ordinated by the Keeper of Extension Services, is now open. Explaining the expansion of Dundee as a major industrial and commercial centre, and showing the growth of certain industries and their associated technology it is targetted successfully at the widest possible audience. During the planning stage detailed

consideration was given to its function as an education resource and there are objects on open display. Another gallery on local and social history is proving extremely popular: there are reconstructions of a Victorian public bar, a grocer's shop and a school classroom. The experienced team in Extension Services is keen and ready to develop good education programmes for all ages linked to these galleries as it already does most effectively with its talks on local history, with its summer walks, its workshops, holiday activities, loan kits, and outreach programmes linked to other museums in Dundee.

Just about everyone in museum education I have talked to has spent a lot of time getting to know local advisers in all sorts of subjects. With the curricular developments in both Primary and Secondary Schools in Scotland I think everyone in museum education – and hopefully in the rest of the museum world in Scotland – is aware of the importance of museums and galleries slotting into the development of new teaching programmes. Several years ago in the then Royal Scottish Museum in Edinburgh, an exhibition *About Face* was devised by education and curatorial staff specifically for educational use, and particularly for the new approach in the Art and Design curriculum. Drawing on the museum's extensive collections, it presented a cross-cultural picture showing how decoration of the face has been and still is an important aspect of human behaviour. Preparation and planning of the exhibition involved not just education staff but teachers and a Curriculum Development Officer in Art and Design and as a result of this co-operation a series of workshops, events and educational experiences took place involving young people. Moray House

College of Education saw that this whole programme might be a useful teaching tool, and the Visual Arts Department combined with the Department of Educational Television to make a video, recording the preparation and use of the exhibition by two schools: this video has already been used in training conferences with some considerable success: it would not have been possible without co-operation and goodwill between education and curatorial staff, local advisory staff and college of education lecturers.

Many museum education professionals are involved in preparing material for Reminiscence Groups of some kind or another. With some $\frac{3}{4}$ million pensioners in Scotland we have a growing market amongst those who are retired but keen to study subjects that interest them now they have the free time. Others have skills and experience that they are willing to offer in exchange for a chance to keep their minds active and alert. Museum education staff are putting together slides and objects which hopefully trigger off memories in a structured and creative way. Further developments of this kind of work are happening in many areas. In Edinburgh a community worker has developed a stimulating programme over several months with some old age pensioners, the local primary school and the National Museum, while in Perth a programme has been set up with the help of the Museum's Education Officer involving reminiscence with some elderly patients suffering from senile dementia. A fascinating project in Arran involves the High School, the Museum and many of the local community, resulting in exhibitions, ceilidhs − you name it! A very encouraging example of cross-generation work.

However the fact is that the vast majority of museums and galleries do not have professional museum educators. But we should not despair. Many lively, imaginative curators are doing wonders. The Smith Art Gallery and Museum at Stirling is an inspiration to all. Without any Education Officer until very recently the keen curatorial staff have organised *Operation Skylark* for several years. Let me read you some of the publicity:

'You are invited to "drop in" on Operation Skylark, a countryside playscheme for 8-12 year olds based at Stirling Smith Art Gallery and Museum. Operation Skylark is being organised jointly by 3 different groups, the Smith Museum, Stirling District Countryside Rangers and the Conservation Volunteers with lots of help from others and local sponsors. Operation Skylark will cater for up to 100 children per day and involve them in such varied activities as crafts, farm visits, plant hunts, camping, orienteering, bird watching and much much more . . . in everything we do we aim to have fun but also to put over a message of learning about and caring for the countryside.'

This was first organised in 1983 for four days during the Stirling Festival as a way of making a contribution to the Festival which involved children. The aims as far as the Museum was concerned − to introduce a new generation of museum users to the recently re-opened Museum in an informal, yet educational way and to show the youngsters that the Museum is an active 'living' centre in the community − were different but complementary to the aims of the Ranger Service and Conservation Volunteers. The project was based in the then unconverted main galleries of the

Museum using the museum grounds and surrounding countryside as much as possible. A typical day included activities such as:

earth magic (environmental games), resist & dye (batik), trailrunning (orienteering), hill walking, winged wonders (bird watching), countryside drama, woodwork for wildlife, clay art, guess who? (making animal masks), spade work for nature, up the wall (painting a mural depicting *Skylark* in action), watch the birdie (nature photography), a mini beast hunt and spinning.

The atmosphere of the project was informal and friendly: several hundred children and their families have been re-introduced to the Museum and the Museum has become involved in the community: a success all round!

Anyone can have ideas but not everyone can *achieve* them. Another inspiring example of imaginative work being thought up and put into effect is again at the Smith Art Gallery and Museum. *The People Tapestry* is a festival of events inspired by 'the rich pattern of ideas, customs and religions woven by the migration of people into Central Region'. It had 3 sections: a description of the history of the movement of peoples, ideas and cultures throughout the world into Central Region, an examination of the lives of 5 families now living in the area and a display of traditional costumes lent by these families.

An essential thread in *The People Tapestry* was an extensive range of activities and information services. 21 activities from poetry to story telling, from videos to drama, from a conference organised by Central Region Community Relations Council to craft workshops, from international cookery sessions to embroidery and egg-painting workshops were laid on and participated in by 1,200 visitors who enjoyed the sharing of a celebration of the multi-cultural community that makes up Central Region today.

This participative approach is exactly what museums should be encouraging: museums should be seen as centres of culture and activity, not as storehouses of objects. They should, as Stirling has done in this example, stimulate an active response from the public.

So what do you do if you're an enlightened Director, with no money for an Education post? Well, you could try a Manpower Services Commission scheme. . . .

I know of at least 2 MSC schemes in museum education, one at the Hunterian Museum in Glasgow, the other at the Scottish Fisheries Museum in Anstruther. I am sure many know of Mr Stan Wood and his fossils at the Hunterian Museum and of the many successful children's workshops associated with Mr Wood. Perhaps fewer know of the gem of a museum at Anstruther. It is housed in several 16th-19th-century buildings grouped round a cobbled courtyard at the harbour end of the fishing port. It is a museum humming with life not least because of an MSC team involved in education who offer tours tailored to fit the teacher's needs; who have produced a video on fishing and on seaweeds; who combine a tour of the museum with a beach walk; who combine experience of fishing (Henry, one of the team, is an ex-fisherman) with an ability to communicate, to breathe life into the past, who manage to rise above the restrictions and difficulties of an MSC programme with its short life and complicated do's and don'ts.

And there are those who move from a MSC scheme into permanent jobs in museum education. The new holder of the museum education post at Perth was originally employed on an MSC scheme at Anstruther. Let me show you some of his ambitions by quoting from a report he recently wrote:

'Education Service Profile
Number of employees = 1.
Employed by District Council but wages are paid by Regional Education Authority.
Annual Budget: £808 . . . other money out of general codes for running costs.
Current rules and responsibilities:
(i) Overall responsibility for educational and recreational services provided by the museum.
(ii) Overall responsibility for publicity and public relations along with the museum curator.
(iii) Advice to other members of staff on aspects of their work related to education and recreation.'

He currently provides an impressive list of loan boxes, talks, handling and discovery sessions, field work programmes, projects linked to curriculum development, publications including a leaflet for a life skills class called 'It's your museum'; and lots of advice! His primary aim is 'to make the greatest possible contribution to the welfare of residents of, and visitors to, Perth and Kinross District by helping Perth and Kinross District Museums to make effective use of their special resources – i.e. the collections, the buildings, staff knowledge and expertise – and meet the particular educational and recreational needs of groups and individuals'.

The Lillie Art Gallery in Milngavie has no resident education officer, but has good working relationships with advisers, local teachers and the museum education staff in Glasgow Museums and Art Galleries. It caters on Saturdays for vast numbers of children in art workshops linked to a wide range of exhibitions, permanent and temporary. The curator has no workroom for children, and little money. Another hazard is the fact that there are no toilets. With the help of 2 art teachers, who have to be paid – which means the children have to pay an entry fee – the Lillie Art Gallery has children participating in art; the workshops are constantly over-subscribed; there is a waiting list; indeed parents have been known to put 2-year old children on the waiting list.

The curator is convinced that these Saturday workshops are an invaluable way of getting the children into the gallery, of exposing them to challenging exhibitions, and of giving them an experience that they do not get in schools. She is making her gallery accessible to children and she sees it as important that children should be active – and seen to be active – in her gallery. She also runs evening classes for adults in practical painting, photography, weaving and embroidery: the gallery is open to the public from 6 pm-9 pm for four evenings a week: please note, other museums and galleries. One of the ways the curator works is to combine with other galleries in the South-West Galleries Association in working closely with the Regional Education Authority's Art Advisers, in pooling resources and working together on specific projects and on material that goes out to schools as preparation for a visit.

As a group the South-West Galleries Association is exploring the possibility of a seconded teacher. Such combination and co-operation would appear to be one way forward for small under-resourced galleries.

At the other end of the country in Aberdeen is the Peacock Printmakers which although without an Education Officer at present, has always seen itself as an 'artist in residence' scheme writ large. The core of its existence has always been to provide artists with facilities to make prints and those who work there see it as part of their job to demonstrate and explain what they are doing to both casual and booked visitors, many of whom are school students. There have always been formal classes and courses right from the start, including evening classes and weekend courses. Again they work closely with a group of teachers and advisers and are full of ideas for new 'Book Table' exhibitions, for a small-scale travelling unit and for exciting link-ups between contemporary artists, schools and original prints.

Some museums combine for discussion on many aspects of their work notably in Fife and in the Borders. The Borders Museum Forum has been meeting informally since 1981/2 and has been turned – with advice and encouragement from the Scottish Museums Council – into a formal organisation. As such it has been running for well over 12 months, has a Curators' Sub-committee which meets regularly, and has already organised several seminars. The Forum held a seminar in May on Museum Education which was attended by some 60 representatives of local councils, museums, stately homes and libraries. We exchanged lots of ideas and opinions, and we talked about difficulties, both practical and philosophical. I was delighted that so many museums, local, private and independent, were concerned about museum education. It was a good opportunity to get feedback, and I hope we sowed a few seeds on increasingly fertile ground.

Education at the National Galleries of Scotland

I cannot possibly talk about museum education and not look at what is happening in the National Galleries of Scotland. Pat FitzGerald, Education Officer, has been in post for two years and has brought the Galleries to life for countless people, children and adults alike. Working most of the time on her own, with the occasional extra person on a week by week contract, Pat produces newsletters, workshops, programmes of activities, study packs, competitions and tea parties. First of all I think I need to quote from Colin Thompson, the Director who appointed her, writing in *Look-in,* the Galleries' newsletter for schools '. . . looking at pictures, understanding and enjoying them, is not a passive business to be contrasted to the activity of painting them yourself. On the contrary, it is an active response to things seen that is of the same nature as the response of the painter at his easel looking at apples on a plate beside him – or considering the still life he is making of them. It can be just as lively and positive in its own way. The two activities should complement each other, like reading books and writing yourself. It calls for an imaginative co-operation between school and art gallery, between the people who have the pictures and the children in their care. That is the aim of our present education programme'.

And what has one education officer managed to do? A very great deal. This year

Antonia Reeve

'Living off the Land' – a
workshop for young visitors
organised by the National
Galleries of Scotland.

National Galleries of Scotland

National Galleries of Scotland

'A hind's daughter' by Guthrie.

'James VI & I' by John de Critz.

the Galleries have been packed with programmes; let's take a look at one or two.

Living off the Land was a selection of paintings from the National Gallery's own collection put together to show what life was like in the Scottish countryside in the 19th century. A fascinating study pack was produced with straightforward, easily understood statements, imaginative suggestions for work and areas for investigation. But there was much more than that. Pat FitzGerald had arranged for four people with completely different interests, experiences, and training to comment on the paintings – and they are quite a revelation!

One example is *The Hind's Daughter* by Sir James Guthrie, painted in 1883. 'She is called a hind's daughter. A hind was a farm worker. From an early age, in the countryside children were expected to join in with work in all kinds of ways. She has obviously been sent out by her mother: "Go and fetch me a cabbage from the garden. Here's the knife and don't cut yourself".'

'She has got a sacking apron on which is known as a brat. It is made from an old sack put round her middle and tied, sometimes with a nail to hold it together. These brats were used when women went to pick potatoes. They pulled the corners round from the side and held it in front of them, just like a basket.'

'Finding any illustrations of farm workers or people fairly well down the social ladder is pleasant, as there aren't many. This painting dates from the 1880s, by which time photographers were at work. Occasionally, they found their way onto farms. Ploughing and farming were of principal interest, probably as much to the people who were

being photographed as to the photographers themselves.'

'This picture is a masterpiece. It is one of a small batch of paintings he did whilst he was living out at Cockburnspath.'

'The girl is totally convincing in her setting. She is standing amongst this muddy patch of cabbages. But there is a sense in which the sky, the cabbages, the trees, the house, the girl – you're meant to think of them as being made of paint. The paint is very thick. It gets just a bit smoother where Guthrie goes from the brown clods to her sacking apron and then it gets slightly smoother again in areas like her head and hands. He isn't really interested in real texture the way Cameron was.'

Probably every reader will pick out something different – and that's what makes this whole experience so stimulating.

With the study packs and these comments available the session began with the children discussing the comforts of today – central heating, cars, supermarkets, televisions, cornflakes and crisps – and trying to imagine what life would be like without all these things. There were heated debates about whether the artists had represented 'real' or 'romantic' views of life 100 years ago. The study packs gave the children the chance to make up their own minds about a number of pictures in the gallery before settling down to workshops where they could write a story about someone in one of the paintings, draw some of the wildlife in the hedgerows or create a vegetable collage.

Another programme, *Figures of Fashion* at the Portrait Gallery, stimulated question after question from schoolchildren. In her preview Pat Fitzgerald writes, 'Princess Diana wears a

'Mad Hatter's Tea Party' at the Scottish National Portrait Gallery.

dress with a revealing neckline and she hits the headlines. Prince Charles, however, makes the front page with a candid comment rather than the candid cut of his lounge suit. 400 years ago it would have been very different. Prince and Princess would have been competing "Figures of Fashion". The Stewarts are our royal "Figures of Fashion".'

In the programme the children were introduced to the 16th-century Stewarts and members of their court. The sessions began with 20 questions from the children (no, Pat couldn't answer them all) and each child who asked a question was rewarded with a dip into the jewellery box which was full of sparklers from a department store. To pull the rather random questions together the children were asked to imagine that James VI had stolen the jewels he had on. Without looking at the paintings the children had to help the police with their enquiries by describing the jewellery, the thief, what he was wearing and so on. Apart from all this excitement there was much dressing up, the inevitable discussion about hygiene . . . and a lot of fun!

All this and a Mad Hatter's competition, the Christmas Story, and dazzling plans for education and the Mary Queen of Scots celebrations in 1987. Last year Timothy Clifford as the new Director of the National Galleries wrote also in *Look-in,* 'I sincerely hope that over the next few years our

Education Department will greatly grow in size and give pleasure and instruction to many millions more of Scottish children and adults . . . with only one full-time member of staff in our Education Department, we know the National Galleries of Scotland is grossly understaffed.' We await news![5]

The Future
But you know, in spite of all this, it is still not good enough because there just are not enough of us. Those of us who do exist should be shouting to the rooftops about what we do. People all over Scotland ought to know about us and what museum education really is so that if their local museum does not have an education officer and these sort of activities, they realise they are missing out. And yet what happens? There's an entire edition of the *Museums Journal* called 'Scottish Issue' and is there an article on museum education? No, although I did find the occasional paragraph and a reference in an article on the work of the Scottish Museums Council where its former Director points out that 'outwith the four cities adequate schools museum services are non-existent. In this area, Scotland lags far behind the rest of the UK[6] . . .'.

Of course we welcome the Miles Report[2] with its emphasis on the crucial role education has to play: many of its recommendations make sense although may I put in a plea that loans to schools are *not* a substitute for a museum visit but rather an appetite-whetter? We welcome the description of the functions of a museum education officer: it is *essential* that education is interpreted in as wide a sense as possible and that the person appointed is not merely a schools officer. But is it appropriate

therefore that only those with proven experience as a successful teacher need apply? I wonder. And is it clear that the Working Party see education staff in museums as on a par with curatorial staff? I wonder.

The educational facility offered by museums to the public asks for no qualifications from its participants. It is open to everyone and equally has a responsibility to everyone, from the serious scholar to those disenchanted with formal education. It is a huge task requiring energy, imagination and commitment. It is an exercise in the art of communication with people of all ages many of whom are often cynical, easily distracted and passive in their expectations. Education in museums is a challenge requiring the co-operation and resources of the institution as a whole.

What then of the future? Should we be planning Discovery Rooms? Probably. Should we be getting more travelling exhibitions on the road? Certainly. Should there not be far more co-operation between the National Museums and Galleries and local museums and galleries to provide education programmes that could be truly national? Without a doubt. Should we not all be planning more informal education, more family events, more leisure learning for all age groups? Yes.

But right now in museums in 1987 there are things we must *all* do: if we do not, we shall miss out on becoming an integral part of education in Scotland:

1.   We need to work out some satisfactory system of getting information to the people who need it, particularly in schools.

2. We need to offer good, challenging education programmes in particular to help develop investigative skills, both for teachers and pupils.

3. We need stimulating exhibitions, displays and galleries to work with: to achieve this we must work as part of a team with curatorial and design staff.

4. We need commitment from Public Relations Staff, if we're lucky enough to have them, to make the Press sit up and take notice of our activities.

5. Most important of all, we need constant communication with teachers, advisers, Curriculum Development Officers and Her Majesty's Inspectors but we also need Directors, Trustees and local authorities to recognise publicly the crucial role education staff have in museums so that we see a significant increase in education staff in museums throughout Scotland.

Sources

1.   At the conference this paper began with a dialogue with a 'Big Mac' box. The questions were taken from an article in an ICOM publication: J. Hennigar-Shuh, 'Talking with teachers about museums in Nova Scotia', *Museum* vol. 144, 1984, pp. 184-9.

2.   Museums and Galleries Commission, *Museums in Scotland,* London, 1986.

3.   Scottish Museums Council, *Scottish Museums and Galleries Guide,* Edinburgh, 1986.

4.   David Clarke, Trevor Cowie and Andrew Foxon, *Symbols of Power at the time of Stonehenge,* Edinburgh, 1985.

5.   Since the time of writing a second permanent post in education has been created and filled.

6.   G. Farnell, 'Promoting Excellence: the work of the Scottish Museums Council', *Museums Journal,* vol. 86, no. 1, June 1986, pp. 50-55.

*Introducing pupils to Degas at
the Burrell Collection.*

Resources for Courses:
Meeting the Needs in Local Museums

Stewart Coulter

Stewart Coulter became Museum Education Officer
for Glasgow Museums and Art Galleries in 1980.
Assistant Education Officer since 1972, he had
previously taught in schools in Northern Ireland
and Peru. He is actively involved in the Group for
Education in Museums.

Glasgow Museums and Art Galleries

Introduction

Museums are one of the most important
repositories for a wide variety of primary
source materials. The objects in the
collections represent the best of man's social,
economic and natural environment. Those
on display are generally the tip of the
iceberg while the reserve collections form
vast reservoirs of untapped resources. The
quantity of artefacts obviously varies
according to the size and type of collection
but museums are all potential resource
centres.

The crucial factors in utilising this material
for school courses are:

1.   awareness by teachers that it is there
and can be used in a variety of ways and

2.   the attitudes of the curators in making it
available and accessible.

It is a two-way communication system and
neither side can rely on the other to always
take the initiative. Where a museum has an
education officer the problem of
communicating is eased but in most of
Scotland's museums there are no such
people. One of the major goals of this
publication is the hope that both sides will
become aware of the potential of museum
collections in the modern school curricula.

In Glasgow we are fortunate to have a well
established Museum Education Service –
since 1941 – funded and administered by
Strathclyde Regional Council Education
Department (Glasgow Division). It is staffed
by teachers who know the educational
system and who are still an integral part of
that system; the Museum Education Officer
is also part of the local advisorate. We have
therefore, direct access to teachers and a
major part of our remit is to assist with
curriculum development. An important
element of this co-operation which has
emerged over the past 20 years has been the
establishment of museum teachers panels.

Groups of school teachers meet museum education staff every 6-8 weeks to discuss developments in their subject areas and to prepare relevant courses using museum material and displays. At various times the panels have consisted of geography, history, biology and art teachers and have been invaluable in promoting and interpreting the collections in relation to the school syllabi.

Course development

I propose to take two examples of our work with schools to show how collections can be used as an integral part of school courses.

1. Standard Grade Art Course

One of the most successful courses was developed and piloted by the Museum Art Panel working with our museum teachers at the Burrell Collection. It was based on Burrell's fine collection of Degas paintings and was intended for use as a Standard Grade Art Course. The main aims were:

(i) to develop the pupil's awareness of the work of Degas through a practical approach

(ii) to develop observational and drawing skills

(iii) to encourage pupils to talk freely about works of art and to increase their confidence in group discussions.

The museum staff prepared a tape/slide programme on the life and work of Degas with teacher's notes on his techniques and a bibliography. One of the teachers on the panel prepared a 10 session course of lessons for use in schools based on Degas' techniques. An important ingredient of the course was a visit to the gallery. During the visit the pupils saw the tape/slide programme on the life and work of the artist and were introduced to the Degas paintings on display. They were involved in a

discussion session on the content, construction and techniques used.

From the gallery the pupils went to the Burrell Collection's activity room where the museum teachers had constructed a set resembling the Paris Opera. Some of the pupils became the dancers or models using costume borrowed from the Scottish Ballet and the set was lit with lights borrowed from the Royal Scottish Academy of Music and Drama (a good example of co-operation between the Arts). The other students became budding Degas and using the materials he used – chalks, pastels etc, they drew from the side of the stage. This work was later expanded during the school sessions and in the school holidays was on public display in the Burrell Collection's courtyard.

The success of this programme which was aimed at secondary level was so great that a modified version was offered to primary schools. It has always been our policy that museum courses should be adaptable for different age groups and learning levels and that the development of artistic skills and critical faculties should be encouraged from an early age.

2. Foundation Level History Course

Another working example of co-operation between museums and schools was prepared by the Museum History Panel as a possible short course with cross-curricular elements, which could later be offered at Foundation level for S3/4 pupils. The panel decided to use the museums as the focus of the course. The working title was 'Discovering Glasgow Museums' and the panel produced a teaching pack which included a short video film, assessment sheets, maps, museum

Degas recreated at the Burrell Collection.

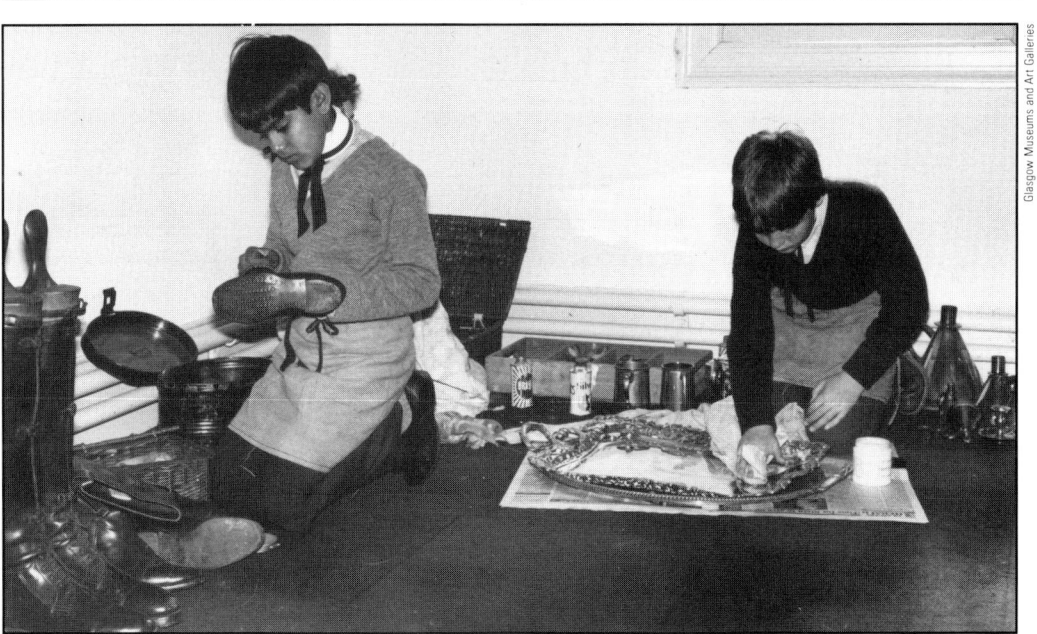

How we used to live below stairs – 1910. Activity programme at Pollok House, Glasgow.

guides and a selection of options for museum visits. The kit suggested a teaching order but it was adaptable to suit the needs of individual teachers and classes. The basic aims of the course were:

(i) to introduce the pupils to their local museums

(ii) to develop an awareness of the work and functions of museums

(iii) to develop an interest in them and through this an interest in their own cultural heritage

(iv) to develop a wide range of general skills including investigative techniques and critical faculties.

The programme was divided into Units including a pre-test section which was designed to assess pupils' knowledge and attitudes about museums at the start of the course. There were then 5 main Units:

UNIT 1 − *The Museums of Glasgow:* aimed at providing a general knowledge of the location and specialisms of Glasgow museums and a general awareness of what a museum is like. The Unit provided (a) a video programme (b) a map of Glasgow showing the location of the museums and a worksheet based on this (c) suggestions for follow-up work.

UNIT 2 − *Planning a Visit to a Museum:* which involved work on travel arrangements, timing controls and decision-making on what they were to see. The Unit provided leaflets on museums, a discussion sheet and further suggestions.

UNIT 3 − *Visiting the Museums:* when the pupils put Unit 2 into action. The main aims of this visit were to arouse interest in displays and to develop a critical awareness of how a museum caters for visitors and displays its collections. These were achieved by means of simple survey sheets. On return to school the pupils used the information as a basis for further discussion.

UNIT 4 − *Behind the Scenes:* this Unit was designed to increase the pupils' knowledge of how a museum collects, conserves and prepares its collection for either display or storage. It included preliminary work in school to familiarise pupils with museum procedures; this included a case study of one subject and how a museum processes it. There was then a further visit to the museum to one of the service departments − a choice was given between (i) taxidermy, (ii) painting conservation, (iii) design and photography, (iv) stores. This helped to spread the work over several departments as it is time-consuming for the museum personnel involved. The most popular choice by the schools involved in the pilot scheme was taxidermy. Pupils prepared questions in advance and the answers to these formed the basis for discussion and written work in school.

UNIT 5 − *Planning a Display:* this final Unit was included to allow pupils to plan a display of their own by applying what they had learned from the previous units and museum visits. The work involved (i) deciding on material to show, (ii) research, (iii) writing labels and/or information sheets, (iv) display techniques.

The teachers who piloted the course were asked to provide detailed assessments and these have been used to modify the Units for future use. By the end of the course the pupils should have a greater awareness of why museums exist and how they work; the problems involved in collecting, conserving and interpretation and should have a more critical approach to display and exhibitions − surely a worthwhile goal for our future rate-paying citizens.

These are two examples of using museums and collections as an integral part of a school course and both could be adapted by most museums. There are many other ways of using specific collections for courses including linking these to school broadcasts which have a high uptake in schools. In recent years the most successful museum/school courses have been for classes following the BBC Television 'Watch' series on Romans, Ancient Egypt and North American Indians; the BBC 'Look, Look and Look Again' series involving portraits and landscapes and the hugely successful ITV series 'How We Used to Live' which has dealt with 3 historical periods – 1874-1887, 1901-1926 and 1933-1953. Museums can provide excellent material for these.

These are some examples of how museum collections can be used as resources for courses. There are many others and every museum, however small, has a contribution to make. The first step in tapping these resources must be closer liaison between museums and the schools; this is a two-way process and curators and teachers must both be made aware of the potential of collections. This publication should help to forge that link.

'Gin yer Finger's haggert, yer cloot keeps out the stang of the brine'.

'Cloots, Creels and Claikin' – Drama on Display

Sandra Keatch

Sandra Keatch teaches Speech and Drama in Upper Deeside Primary Schools in Grampian. Her innovative work with the Mobile Theatre Group in Aberdeen Maritime Museum has been a textbook example of how drama in the museum context has an important part to play in museum education.

Mobile Theatre is a team of Primary School Drama teachers employed by Grampian Regional Council's Education Department. They are released from teaching duties, one day a week, in order to devise, release and perform Theatre in Education experiences for Primary School pupils in the Grampian Region.

As part of the centenary celebrations of the Aberdeen Art Gallery, Mobile Theatre was approached by the Aberdeen Maritime Museum with a view to a 'one-off' presentation. The result was 'Cloots, Creels and Claikin' which was performed weekly in the Museum throughout 1985.

'Cloots, Creels and Claikin' was a living-history experience for twelve-year old children in Grampian Region. In an enactment of fisherfolk life on the east coast of Scotland one hundred years ago, the children learned how fisherfolk worked, lived and loved.

The literature used in the research for the project was borrowed from the Grampian Schools Library Service, the costumes were borrowed from the Council's Costume Wardrobe and the props were supplied by the Maritime Museum. Only one original net mending needle could be found so the eight others used in the project were bought from the Museum Shop!

Primary Schools in Grampian are familiar with the work of Mobile Theatre who have been visiting schools for very many years. That the schools would now be visiting the Mobile Theatre would be something new . . . it would cost the school bus fares to start with . . . but the novelty of some drama happening in the town's new museum meant that there was a very high response to the initial offer of the programme. Schools were invited to apply for a booking and a list of bookings was compiled, up to three months in advance. Mobile Theatre sent the schools preliminary notes about 'Cloots, Creels and Claikin' and gave suggestions for follow up work. Class teachers were requested to organise their classes, maximum 33 pupils (to fit the confines of the Museum) into four groups. In preparation for the day, the children were asked to prepare a suitable period item, musical or spoken, as a contribution to an entertainment at a fisher engagement party.

On the day, the children were met at the Maritime Museum by a member of the Mobile Theatre staff. Museum staff helped with the removal and storage of coats. While the children were being briefed on what they were to be involved in, four characters appeared in full costume. Let the characters introduce themselves.

'Aye, aye, bairns, I'm Mrs Nancy Main, but abody in this village jist cries me, "Nan," so you can jist cry me Nan an a. Noo, I've some fishies that need guttin so I'll be wantin some help wi them. Min, ye'll hae tae cloot yer fingers wi the strippies o auld floor sacks first. Here's my mairriet dauchter, Sarah.'

'Aye, aye, I'm Sarah Bochals, an my man's awa at sea of noo. I'm packin a kist wi gifts for ma sister that's gettin mairriet neist week, so you can see a the bonny things I've tae pit in it.'

'Noo, I'm Jessie Flett, Nan's sister an I wark at the nets. Ye see, I'm a widow, an since I hinna got a man tae gang tae sea for me, I jist hae tae dae fit I can tae mak a livin, but fyles, I get affa ahint masel, so I'd be rale gled if ye'd look by an gie me a haun.'

'Good morning, young ladies, young gentlemen, my name is Mrs Anne Duthie, wife of Mr John Duthie, of the famous ship building firm of Duthie and Sons. In considering employment here, let me tell you that you are applying for a post with one of Aberdeen's finest and most respected ship building firms.'

The other characters did not appear at the Museum, but later, as the dramatic content of the storyline emerged.

Though the layout of the Museum may at first appearances seem unsuitable for things theatrical 'Cloots, Creels and Claikin' was specially designed to fit the Museum. The four characters positioned themselves in four different areas of the Museum, and the groups of children visited each one in turn.

In the Trawling and Fishing Gallery, Nancy and Sarah had their 'cottages'. With Nancy, the children heard about the conditions of work in the herring industry one hundred years ago. They practised 'clooting' their fingers and helped to gut and clean some real fish (kindly supplied and delivered free of charge, every week, by an inshore fish selling company). The intimacy of this experience necessitated the use of one air freshener on the warmer days! With Sarah, they helped to unpack a 'kist' that contained the possessions of a relative who was drowned at sea. Then the kist was repacked with period household goods in preparation for Sarah's sister's wedding. The 'claikin' began when Nancy called Sarah to come 'ben' to her cottage and both groups of children rallied to hear of another character called Grizzle. Grizzle was considered an 'unlucky person' and here the children learnt of fisherfolks' strong beliefs in superstitions.

In the Picture Gallery with a clear space in the middle of the floor, Jessie laid out a large fishing net that was in need of repair. Having heard a detailed account of the damage caused by the Great Gale of 1876 which claimed her husband's life, the children were given a quick lesson in net mending which they attempted using proper net needles.

Fingers and thumbs at net mending? The children visited Mrs Duthie for their job interview and a taste of Victorian town life.

Girls were interviewed for the job of laundrymaid and had to sew a seam. The boys had to copy some handwriting to prove their ability to write in the large Duthie ledger book. The original ledger book lay open upon the table where the children stood to answer Mrs Duthie's questions. Mrs Duthie played a strict disciplinarian and no child dared put a foot out of place in the Duthie room. And just as well, as the Duthie room, representing the Victorian office of the famous shipbuilding family, must be one of the Aberdeen Maritime Museum's showpieces. Lift anything and the alarm bells ring. But forewarned is forearmed – 'Dinna pit yer sticky fingers oan her bonny furniture,' said Jessie beforehand. The alarm bells never rang.

The setting was unique and the drama was carefully planned around some excellent characters and an interesting storyline and 'amid the picters and the boaties, the trawl nets and the creels,' invariably there were children who were totally enthralled and involved. Wrote one child afterwards in a thank-you letter: 'I thought the actors were very good as firstly I thought they were completely real.'

Wrote another: 'I thought I was going to a museum, but that was an adventure.'

The adventure was not over. After 40 minutes, the groups reunited and walked about 500 yards up the street, led by the fishwives, to the Aberdeen Children's Theatre building, which was, for the purposes of the day, furnished and decorated to represent a Fisherman's Mission Hall. Here the children were to take part in a 'Beukin Party', which is a fisher engagement party. The children were given simple pieces of costume to help them enter the spirit and also they were given an old penny with which they would pay the fiddlers at the end.

Already, upstairs in the hall, the fiddlers were playing. Two retired people played every week at the 'beukin party'. Dressed in full costume, they loved to chat in character to the children and this added yet another dimension to the attempt to reconstruct the past. During the party, the children were involved in traditional singing, dancing, recitations and both religious and good luck ceremonies. However, Grizzle Duggie burst in on the gathering, unwelcome and uninvited. After threats of spell-making, curses, accusations and counter accusations, peace was finally restored, when it was discovered that she had lost a fisher love from the same boat that had claimed Jessie's husband. At heart, Grizzle was a tragic soul from a farmer family who had been a victim of too much close knit, fisher village gossip. As the party closed everyone sang a Scots version of 'The Lord's my Shepherd', then on leaving, shook hands with the bride and groom (two children pre-selected by their teacher to play the special roles). The guests left happily and hopefully, enlightened.

There was a story.

There were a few traditional Scottish words to learn.

There were some new skills to try.

There was a living example portraying fisher ways and customs.

There was an illustration of fisher relationships with other communities.

There was a visit to the Aberdeen Maritime Museum where there had been things made available to touch as well as see.

The Maritime Museum creates a feeling that

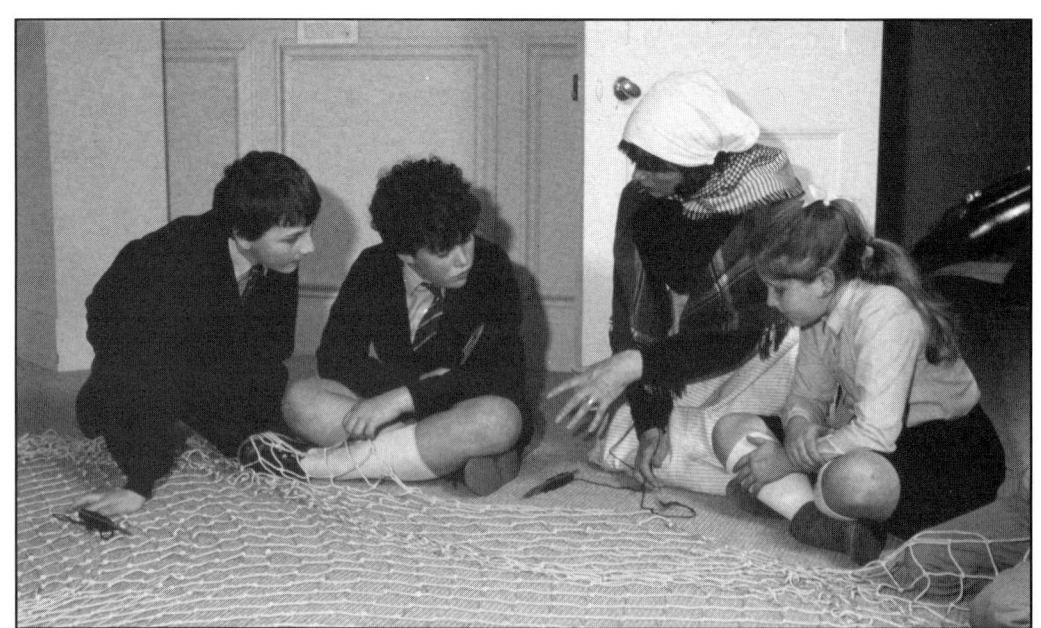

'Noo, is anybody here corrie-fisted?'

'Noo, here's yer knife. Aff wi the heid and noo the tail'.

80

'Aince this Kist belanged tae Jess's man, noo it's for happier times'.

'Wha is my shepherd, weel I ken ...'

the past is something special and to be respected. The Mobile Theatre team, being teachers for the most part of the week, understood that it was often difficult for children to imagine the past in relation to themselves. In 'Cloots, Creels and Claikin' the Mobile Theatre Team tried to bring some elements of times gone by straight home to the hearts of the children. The 'fishwives' shared a few moments of their 'lives' with the children and through the playful interaction between both parties, it was hoped that the children became aware of how fisher life of 1885 might have affected them.

In linking to the primary school curriculum, the programme worked in a number of ways. Some classes used the visit as a starting point for a project on fishing or Aberdeen, whilst for others, it was used as a high spot at the end of such a project. Where a school was already committed to theme studies far removed from the realms of 'Cloots, Creels and Claikin', at least a visit to the Maritime Museum, complete with an experience of 'Cloots, Creels and Claikin' would certainly make a valuable starting point for a lesson in local or environmental studies.

Judging from the 'claik' as the children left the building, they found plenty to talk about. The head teacher of a school south of Stonehaven, where there is still a distinct division between fisher and farmer folk, told me afterwards that the project had stimulated a lively discussion about 1885 compared to 1985. The consensus of opinion was, that as far as basic attitudes were concerned, not a lot had changed.

Both Mobile Theatre and Museum staff received examples of written follow up work. We received pieces recounting the day out, proper thank-you letters and letters of criticism and appreciation. Some children wrote as if to their mother recounting their experiences 'at the fish' or 'in-service' at the Duthies. One school wrote their work in the Doric, their local dialect.

*   *   *

Walker Road School,
Aberdeen.
20th June, 1985.

Dear Sarah,

I am writing to thankyou for a lovely morning. I really enjoyed myself. I felt like I was taken back in time. You all seemed so happy even with all the work. It was very interesting to hear all your superstitions.

Tell Nan I am still practising with a cloot I made. I'll maybe get it right yet.

I don't think I have got the knack of making nets. Jessie was very patient with us and I wished I could have helped more.

Mrs Duthie is quite a good person. I got a surprise to hear how long a laundry maid works. I don't think I would make a good laundry maid.

I especially liked the party. I did get a piece of shortbread and I had a dream. I felt very sorry for Grizzle. She seemed so sad. I hope Jane and Christopher will be happy.

Thankyou again for a lovely time.

Yours sincerely,
Lisa L. Taylor.
Midmar School,
Sauchen,
Aberdeenshire.
14th November.

*   *   *

Dear Mr. Biggs,

Thankyou very much for letting us go to 'Cloots, Creels and Claikin' at the Maritime Museum. I think it was very realistic. I liked the lady who was gutting the 'real' fish. I liked it when you had to say ma'm to Mrs Duffy. Sarah and Bill got a surprise when they knew that they were bride and groom. I think that your performance was very good. We went to the Maritime Museum before but it was better this time because people were showing you what it was like a hundred years ago.

Yours sincerely,
Russell Beveridge.

*   *   *

There were suggestions for drama work in the teachers' notes, e.g. Choose a certain fisher superstition and make up a short play based on that superstition e.g. it's considered unlucky for a fisherman to get his feet wet before a day's fishing; show how the fisher of 1885 kept his feet dry, but what happened the day he got his feet wet.

One school made a video of their interpretation of fisherlife in their village 100 years ago acting out the scenes 'on location'!

Knowing the integrated nature of the primary school curriculum, 'Cloots, Creels and Claikin' was probably used as a starting point for lessons in other subjects, but the Mobile Theatre team have not been in a position to assess this.

Reactions were favourable all round towards the project and having worked with the Museum, Mobile Theatre is certainly much more aware of the benefits of hopping the fences of regional departments with a view to sharing resources.

Let one of the final comments come from the headmistress of a large and traditional Aberdeen school.

*   *   *

'History was really brought to life for all of us and the members of the public who were in the Museum with us were enthralled by your staff. It is a great pity this couldn't continue throughout the tourist season. It would prove a great attraction and an education.'

*   *   *

Indeed the Maritime Museum didn't have to close its doors to the public to allow the drama to take place. As part of the living history experience, a retired fisherman once joined in with Nancy as she told tales of hardship, an American tourist tried his hand at net mending and two women returned a few weeks later for a second helping.

'Cloots, Creels and Claikin' ended its run in December, 1985. Mobile Theatre are back on the move, touring schools with a new programme and the Maritime Museum may be a little quieter on Wednesdays now that the 'fishwives' have gone. Surely out of it all, there was something for everyone to think about, to remember and perhaps treasure for a time to come.

'Bubbles', The Children's Museum, Boston.

New Approaches to Science: In the Museum or Outwith the Museum?

Stephen Feber

Stephen Feber is Chief Executive of the Children's
Museum's Eureka! project, one of the most exciting
museum education developments currently taking
place in U.K. He was formerly Assistant Curator of
the Museum of Childhood at Sudbury Hall in
Derbyshire.

Museums are increasingly being spoken of as institutions where 'informal learning' takes place[1, 2]. Despite the title of this publication I will use the word 'learning' rather than 'education' because the latter implies a programme of instruction, a syllabus and a certain formality, and museums, after all, provide opportunities to learn, but are not schools. Learning also implies an everyday activity and this is appropriate in this context. If I asked whethere you had ever learnt something by *doing* as opposed to listening, reading or watching, you might well reply that you had, perhaps citing a particular hobby you practised or a skill you had acquired. But if I asked whether you still knew how to play you might wonder at the relevance of the question; surely play is for *children*? On this point we might have to exchange 'experiment' for play, to make the idea of testing hypotheses and proceeding by trial and error more acceptable. If you are with me thus far you will be familiar with all the ingredients of the new exhibition initiatives usually grouped under the rubrics 'hands on' or 'interactive'; informal learning, doing, and playing or experimenting. In the new techniques these basic processes are deployed in a public setting in the belief that an enjoyable process is not the antithesis of a worthwhile and serious result.

I should make a few points about the title of my paper; 'New Approaches to Science: In the Museum or Outwith the Museum'. 'New approaches' is really a misnomer; although they are only just beginning to appear in this country they owe their impetus to experiments carried out in Canada and North America over the past twenty years, most notably at three institutions: the Ontario Science Centre, the San Francisco Exploratorium and the Boston Children's Museum. I will speak mainly about the last two. We must remember that Oppenheimer, founder of the Exploratorium, visited the Science Museum in South Kensington, the Palais de la Decouverte in Paris and the Deutsches Museum in Munich during the sixties when he was thinking about starting his own venture[4]. It is important to stress the common intellectual property as much as the originality in these developments.

Although three of the UK Science and Technology Centre projects are associated with museums ('Launch Pad' at the Science Museum, London, Greater Manchester Museum of Science and Industry and Merseyside Museums) the relationship between interactive exhibition methods and the museum is by no means fully worked out. 'Launch Pad' for example, is in many ways a technology centre within a museum with a vestigial relationship to the traditional galleries. I take the second part of the title 'In the Museum or Outwith the Museum' to refer to the issue of the institutional base that has nurtured these techniques and the impact they will have on the social and cultural role of museums.

The motives for the introduction of different exhibition techniques in the UK are various but they are certainly part of a general feeling that as science and technology have permeated our lives more and more thoroughly, they have become less and less accessible. We certainly once had a popular scientific culture in this country. In 1828 The London Magazine could report this rather alarming picture:

'In every town, nay almost in every village, there are learned persons running to and fro with electric machines, galvanic troughs, retorts, crucibles and geologists' hammers.'

Knowledge of science was seen both as a valuable cultural pursuit and a means of social advancement[5]. In Manchester, the Literary and Philosophical Society chose science as the preferred intellectual genre because it had possibilities as 'polite knowledge, as rational entertainment, as theological instruction, as professional occupation, as technological agent, as value transcendent pursuit and as intellectual ratifier of a new world order'[6]. Above all

science was accessible; it was seen as one of the motor forces of the new industrial order and its importance was reflected in a wide availability of popular scientific literature.

Today, projects like 'Launch Pad'[7] have been funded by the Leverhulme Trust and by the Department of Trade and Industry as part of a conscious cultural intervention to raise the perceived value of science, engineering and technology. Such thinking is linked, in more or less explicit ways, with desire to improve industrial performance and competitiveness. There are equally powerful broad scale ambitions at work which seek to widen the cultural base to include science and technology and to make specific extensions of the educational provisions for school children. Whatever the motive, participation and easy access are the keynotes of interactive exhibition strategies; whether we are now going to see a 'hands on' learning centre in every town and a science playground in every village, remains to be seen.

What then is an 'interactive' exhibit? By definition it is not inactive; it does not present a fixed structure like a cased exhibit; nor yet merely reactive, as might be so with a push button device where a single action produces a single consequence. It is an object or construction that can be varied by the visitor; the interactive exhibit usually allows variable inputs and consequently variable outcomes; the best exhibits genuinely prompt and sustain sequences of exploration, experiment, conceptualisation and re-experiment. Exhibits can vary a good deal in the amount of freedom they allow the visitor for trial and error but very often there is a pay-off or reward in using them. This intrinsic reward, usually the completion

*Pump Kit' – Launch Pad,
Science Museum, London.*

of a sequence or initiation of an event of some kind, is a powerful motivator in the discovery process. The water pump exhibit at the Launch Pad is a good example.

You are invited to assemble a pump that has been created in a way that allows it to be broken down into constituent parts. It is possible to vary the construction and to experiment with the fit of the components; it is even possible to assemble the pump with one part incorrectly fitted so that the pump will work but, not very efficiently. Of course the aim is to assemble it correctly and for this there is the pay-off of being able to pump water with great satisfying splashes.

Oppenheimer has commented;

'In some ways an exhibit resembles a play or musical composition. A tension is built up by something in the exhibit that elicits curiosity, or an interesting task, or a lovely effect, and then the tension is resolved as the result of an aesthetic or intellectual pay off. If either component is missing, either the creation of the tension or its relief, the exhibit is unsatisfactory. The creation of tension should not involve flamboyance or the high signal strength of traditional advertising. It should be a quiet affair, for if the exhibit shouts "Hey come and Look at Me" the museum will become impossibly tiring for visitors'[8].

The Bubbles exhibit at the Exploratorium and the Boston Children's Museum (now copied in many other locations) is another example of an exhibit that includes suspense, an aesthetic element and a final reward. It is successful not only because it produces genuinely beautiful results but because the learning curve is steep but easy. The visitor can move from spectator to expert in a few seconds.

'Sun' is a classic interactive Exploratorium exhibit; it allows the visitor to see the controlled dispersion, recombination and redirection of light 'it is in effect a sort of paint palette for sunlight . . . it is an art piece by Robert Miller (and) it also works as a science exhibit[9]. In the exhibit, sunlight is collected from the roof and directed via a series of prisms and mirrors onto a large screen. The combination of reflection, and dispersion produces beautiful colours and effects. Shadows and forms are produced as visitors move either side of the screen and the exhibit truly shows the meeting of the scientific and the aesthetic.

Interactive exhibits can produce an exhibition with a quite different feeling to the traditional linear or narrative exhibition; the object in the case has gone, as has the label as muted proclamation. Visitors can move at random and at their own pace through exhibition areas, many of whose themes are presented in a number of ways to create repetition and variation. Oppenheimer again:

'We have 18 different examples of resonance and standing waves. There are resonances in air columns, in strings and ropes, in metal plates and rubber membranes, in rods and springs, in water and in mechanical wave machines.'[10]

This principle is clearly shown in the Boston Children's Museum's 'Raceways' exhibition where aspects of kinetic and potential energy are explored. In effect such informal environments provide 'multi sensory' experiences that allow a range of interactions; looking, touching, listening, talking and reading. This is an important element in increasing the sociability of the visit; visitors learn much more from watching each other, simply because the process of discovery is on view.

It will come as no surprise to learn that such exhibition environments are enormously popular. Nor, within limits, is the popularity of involvement culturally specific to North America. 'Launch Pad', which stands in the Exploratorium tradition, has been a great success and the Ontario Science Centre's 'Science Circus', which has toured 'hands on' exhibits to Japan, Britain and the Middle East, has found great similarity in response from place to place. This is an important point because it appears that interactive exhibition environments tap fundamental aspects of human social and cognitive behaviour.

Visiting an exhibition is a particular kind of social event, at once private and public, formal and informal. In fact watching the crowd at a museum, at least on the surface, is like watching the crowd in a shopping centre; people wander at their own pace; lighting upon something of particular interest or skipping whole sections; they browse and explore. It is such a characteristic activity in public places that it appears to be an expression of natural exploratory behaviour. And museums and shopping centres also appear to fulfil a profound need to congregate, to be with others. Institutions that have provided interactive exhibitions have understood this, perhaps unconsciously, and allowed visitors to range freely, explore and be gregarious. Visitors to the Boston Children's Museum will comment on the friendliness of the Museum – the warmth of welcome given by the staff is undoubtedly an important factor – but it may be that they find the environment comfortable because it fits their behaviour. It feels good because it makes human sense.

Secondly, at the cognitive level, interactive exhibitions have at their heart an invitation to play which is seductive to young and old. Fundamentally, the playing visitor is using experimental strategies; forming hypotheses, testing them, rejecting some ideas and retaining others; this appears to be as satisfying to the adult as the child. It is also undoubtedly the reason interactive exhibits are so appropriate for science subjects.

Thirdly, providing a number of different experiences that develop a theme acknowledges that visitors come with widely differing propensities to learn. Institutions like the Exploratorium and the Children's Museum have recognised, and acted upon, something most museums have always known; that their audiences come in a range of ages, sizes, inclinations and abilities.

As participation increases and learning is foregrounded so the role of staff changes, indeed specially trained staff on the exhibit floor are a key element in making these exhibition environments work. Boston recruits new 'interpreters' every year and puts them through its own training programme. They are far removed from the uniformed attendants in our major museums, and learn not just information about the subjects the Museum covers but how to deal with the public, how to facilitate learning for children and parents and how to help school groups. They are also coached in the subtle arts of visitor management; having been taught programmes of activities that work well for crowds of people.

But why provide such exhibits? Oppenheimer and Bernie Zubrowski, science developer at the Boston Children's Museum, share the same fundamental belief that by giving visitors particularly vivid experiences

'Raceways', The Children's Museum, Boston.

they will be able to make conceptual connections between the gallery experience and the everyday world. Oppenheimer again:

'Museum experiences most certainly can influence the way in which people perceive their subsequent experiences. We hope, for example, that when visitors who have been to the Exploratorium see a rainbow or look at the blue sky or see strange shafts of light when they squint, they will remember the Exploratorium and say to themselves, "Aha! What I am seeing is like the exhibits at the Exploratorium – the behind of light in Glass Beads, the scattering of light by the cylinder of gelatin in Blue Sky or the Diffraction of light around my eyelashes in Diffraction. I saw those exhibits on the mezzanine of the Exploratorium".'[11]

Zubrowski:

'What I hope children will gain from playing with bubbles is the realisation that there are many patterns in both natural and human-made phenomena, and that such patterns are a vital part of science. . . . The shapes that bubbles take are similar enough to encourage the search for patterns, yet they are always different enough to arouse anticipation.'

Launch Pad has slightly different, but related, expectations to do with attitude change; 'the success of Launch Pad will be measured by the changes it makes in the people who come to it (and much of that will be non-objective learning)'.[12]

To prompt the visitor to see analogies, ask questions and perhaps feel better about a subject formerly found to be intimidating – these all seem perfectly reasonable aims. There is no high expectation about the transfer of 'knowledge' to the visitor; that he or she might come away 'knowing', for example, that angular momentum is the product of a moment of inertia and angular velocity. Nevertheless the visitor may well have had the direct physical experience of the effect (say on the turntable exhibit at the Exploratorium) and can use this 'experiential base' either to coalesce previous experiences or as an element in future learning. Yet we should not pitch expectations about the kind of learning in such exhibitions too low; there is evidence to suggest that under the right circumstances objective learning can take place.

Minda Borun, who is one of the more interesting researchers on learning in public exhibitions in America, has looked at the cognitive and affective results of children and adults using 'interactive' exhibits. In her most recent study 'Planets and Pulleys'[13] she examined the relationship between a class visit to the simple machines gallery at the Franklin Institute in Philadelphia and a class lesson on the same subject area. In the main, her view was that participatory museum displays can and do teach science:

'Regardless of the type of cognitive measure employed (i.e. verbal, visual or performance) the data unequivocally support the hypothesis that fifth and sixth graders visiting a museum exhibit score significantly higher on a test of science content than students in a control group.'[14]

She also found that the exhibits she chose to look at, simple machines, were more effective at communicating science principles than in teaching vocabulary or suggesting practical applications. She went on:

'The more important findings of the study however, are in the affective domain. As hypothesised, the affective data indicate that the museum exhibit is perceived as far more enjoyable and interesting than a classroom lesson. This is true whether the basis of comparison is a museum lesson or the students' own school classes. . . . More specifically, a large proportion of students who visited the exhibit indicated a desire to learn more about simple machines.'[15]

We should be careful about generalising from these findings; Borun was using exhibits conceptually appropriate to the age group under test and in a gallery with a single theme. But although school groups were the subjects, there is nothing in the study to suggest that other groups or individuals would not benefit from using the gallery in a similar way. The notion that either a vivid or unusual experience, a skill newly acquired or the 'Aha!' moment when a sudden connection is made could be the foundation for an important learning event has been articulated in the literature of developmental psychology. The long term effects of such moments in exhibitions are notoriously difficult to test but we do have anecdotal evidence as to their efficacy[16]. Increasingly, the affective component is being recognised as important in mainstream education; the Association for Science Education's Science Teacher's Handbook, for example, lists an affective dimension amongst its goals for science education. Indeed other points on the list, content, context and process could also be covered in an interactive science exhibition[17, 18].

Increasing the sociability of the visit to an exhibition, the levels of participation, the freedom to learn and the degree of enjoyment seems all very well but what has it to do with museums? Not necessarily anything at all; as we have seen, some of the work in developing interactive techniques has taken place outside museums in science centres. And science centres may have allowed the essential intellectual freedom for new ideas to develop. A museum could preserve its traditional cultural function of gathering the evidence of social and natural change, which is essential facet of a civilised society, and never trouble with an interactive exhibition. Collection, preservation and research could proceed with the public interpretation of the process taking the form of the scholarly exhibition. There are, of course, many examples of just this activity up and down the country.

However, there is now good evidence to suggest that the scholarly case/object/label exhibition with simple interpretive means but a high information content creates poor learning opportunities for the bulk of the museum audience[19, 20, 21]. If museums are to take seriously their social role as popular learning centres then they need to become better communicators. But are museums appropriate venues for interactive exhibitions? I would argue that they are. The conflict between the interactive exhibition and the museum – between the specimen and the device, is more apparent than real. There is no reason why interactive exhibits and museum objects should not be mixed in a gallery; not only would they be mutually informative but specimens can very often provide a 'real world' context for the purpose-built exhibit. A criticism that can be levelled at the science centre of the Exploratorium variety is precisely that insufficient contextual information is supplied. Nor need interactive devices be confined to science and technology exhibitions; one can imagine interactive exhibits on perspective or colour theory in an art gallery. The Boston Children's Museum, for example, has pioneered participatory exhibitions on subjects as diverse as the urban environment, handicap and death. And it is a 'real' museum with some 50,000 objects in the collection.

Should this trend develop in the UK, and I feel sure it will, then the consequences could be quite profound. The example of Boston is important, not just because it makes good educational sense: in listening to its audience, freeing itself from reliance on museum objects as the sole content of its exhibitions, and in experimenting with different means of communication, Boston has truly begun to re-define the role of the museum and extend it to become a learning centre. If this lead is followed we will come to see the interactive device and the specimen as two kinds of museum object – that which is preserved and that which is used up in the learning process – they will exist in galleries with a reciprocal learning effect. To make this change in the balance of museums activities three major changes will have to happen: first, the collecting, conserving and research role of museums will become less public, though no less essential; secondly, this will support and inform a 'front of house' where the emphasis is on communication handled by a multi-disciplinary department[22, 23]; thirdly, exhibit floor staff will change their function from guardianship to facilitators of learning.

What then are the prospects for the take up of these ideas? In the short to medium term I expect to see numbers of museums experimenting with interactive techniques. They are too seductive and exciting to be missed and the immediate pay-back for the staff who create them is great. Science and technology centres will continue to grow and flourish although it is likely that they will initially mostly start from an existing institutional base. Independent operations, like the Buxton Micrarium, will probably remain a rarity, if only because of the difficulty of starting them. Science-based adventure playgrounds have already been built in America and India and it can only be a matter of time before local authorities follow suit in the UK. There will undoubtedly be fringe commercial growths, emanating from the theme park world, which will decrease the learning content in favour of high throughput of visitors. I think the spread of broad-based learning centres for children like the Children's Museum project will be slower, if only because there are fewer readily available models. Also the American models suggest the creation of realistic contextual learning environments for young children and these are expensive to design and build compared to interactive science centre devices.

Embracing new methods of communication and fulfilling their roles as popular learning centres, as well as centres of learning, need not threaten the traditional activities of museums, but if the desire to communicate is to be translated into effective exhibitions it needs to seize the staff at every level; the cultural changes within museums could be profound.

Sources

1. Brian N. Lewis, 'The Museum as Educational Facility', *Museums Journal,* 3, 1980.
2. Richard Chase, 'Museums as Learning Environments', *Museum News,* September/October, 1975.
3. The Science Museum's 'Launch Pad', the Children's Museum's 'Eureka!' project, the Bristol Exploratory, science and technology centres or exhibitions at Winchester, Manchester (G.M.M.S.I.), Jodrell Bank, the Buxton Micrarium and Cardiff Techniquest.
4. See – 'Exploration and Culture, Oppenheimer Receives Distinguished Service Award', *Museum News,* November/December, 1982.
5. David Layton, Angela Davey and Edgar Jenkins, 'Science for Specific Social Purposes: Perspectives on Adult Scientific Literacy,' *Studies in Science Education,* 13, 1986, pp. 27-52.
6. Thackray, 'Natural Knowledge in Cultural Context: the Manchester Model,' *The American Historical Review,* vol. 79, 1974, pp. 672-709.
7. Anthony Wilson and Sue Watt, *Launch Pad,* Science Museum, London, 1986.
8. Frank Oppenheimer, 'Exhibit Conception and Design,' Paper presented to Meeting of International Commission on Science Museums, Monterey, Mexico, 1980.
9. 'Recipe No. 1' in *San Francisco Exploratorium Cookbook No. 1.*
10. Oppenheimer, op. cit. (note 8).
11. Oppenheimer, op. cit. (note 8).
12. Anthony Wilson, 'Test Bed and Launch Pad, Interaction at the Science Museum', *View* no. 23, Spring, 1985.
13. Minda Borun, Barbara Flexer, Alice Casey and Lynn Baum, *Planets and Pulleys, Studies of Class Visits to Science Museums,* Franklin Institute, 1983.
14. Borun et al., op. cit. (note 13).
15. Borun et al., op. cit. (note 13).
16. Anthony Wilson, op. cit. (note 12).
17. *Science 5-16: A Statement of Policy,* HMSO, 1985.
18. John Nellist and Brian Nichol, eds, *Science Teacher's Handbook,* 1986, pp. 1-9.
19. H. Shettel, M. Butcher, T. S. Cotton, J. Northrup, D. Slough, *Strategies for Determining Exhibit Effectiveness,* American Institute for Research, Pittsburgh, 1968.
20. Wolf and Tymitz, *East Side, West Side, Straight Down the Middle: A Study of Visitor Perceptions of 'Our Changing Land' the Bicentennial Exhibit,* National Museum of Natural History, Smithsonian Institution, Washington D.C., 1979.
21. Brian N. Lewis, op. cit. (note 1).
22. There are a number of different models for exhibition development, both the Exploratorium and Boston have used a team approach to design and production (both use their own fabrication departments).
23. See also Roger Miles, 'Exhibitions, Management for a Change', in *The Management of Change in Museums,* National Maritime Museum, London, 1985.

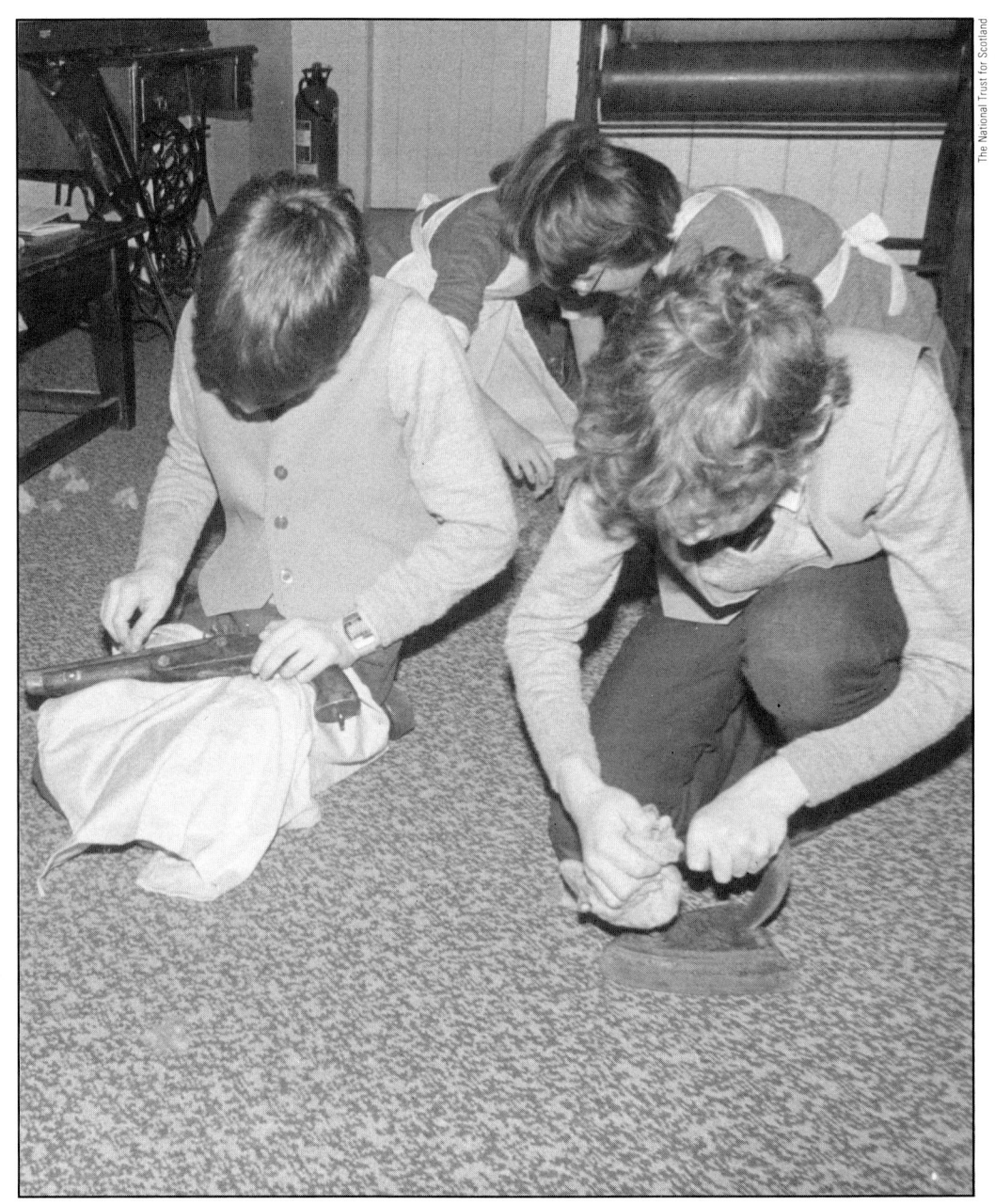

Schools project 'Situation Vacant', Culzean Castle, Ayrshire.

The Souter, the Plaid and the Muckle Wheel: Children and the National Trust for Scotland

Marista Leishman

Marista Leishman was until 1987 Head of the National Trust for Scotland's Education Dept; she is now Director of the Insite Trust, which is a training service for guides in historic houses and museums.

Sometime ago I was attending a meeting in London to talk about applicants for the Sandford Award. I will say a little more about the Award later, but it is given to Houses and Museums which have conspicuously brought in new and imaginative ideas for education. Through much of that afternoon I argued strenuously against the use of worksheets for teaching purposes as one House and Museum after another produced yet another unconvincing batch of papers. I was not, I may say, having trouble pressing my point since there was plenty of support and others more competent to argue than I.

Next day, my business completed, I had two hours to fill and went to the National Gallery. Perhaps the motivation was not all that high – I had read stringent criticism of their worksheets and I was curious. I picked up my copies and homed in on a little knot of activity in the corner of one gallery.

Instantly I received a batch of impressions:

These children, aged between 7 and 9, were at home.

They were working in an intimidating building but were not intimidated by it.

They were unattended by any adult. The question of discipline didn't arise because discipline was rising out of an unexpressed group consensus.

From which it follows that they were totally absorbed. So too, were some adults who watched in kindly amusement.

Pictures were a game. The enjoyment was visible.

I need hardly go on to say that these children were learning – and learning fast. I may say this was a mixed experience for me. Here, under my very nose, was the goal to which in all teaching in the National Trust for Scotland we had aspired, being achieved by a route which we had pronounced as quite discredited.

And so I am slightly uneasy because I thought I was planning to write, without reservation, what, in my view, was the objective in education in the Historic House, and equally without reservation what was the route by which that goal was to be reached. Mercifully I can still endorse the first: that on-site learning is well and thoroughly done when freedom and enjoyment and a spirit of enquiry are all present; but I have to add to my surprise that worksheets may be one of the routes. That is, if they are as well and as humorcusly and non-reverentially done as those in the National Gallery. And that is too, if we do not assume to ourselves a role which is heavily didactic. We are here to open doors, enlarge experience; but not to set tests and award marks. We are not in business to teach – as much as to back up teaching.

There are different ways of going about this back up. Some of them are by way of the muckle wheel, the plaid and the souter. That's not very clear is it? It's another way of saying that a Historic House chiefly offers its valuables for learning, and it offers places – the impression of place that makes an indelible memory. And it's about people – not just the people of history and ghosts of the past, but the people you meet there and who interpret it for you and make it live.

The first one, the things of the house, does not seem to provide a very promising start. 'Please Do Not Touch' says the label and we are condemned to looking at what we long to handle as well. But – looking *should* be enough. After all, culturally we are

programmed to seeing at the expense of touching and feeling and smelling. This emphasis is no new thing, for it is to be found rooted deeply in everyday language. 'Oh, I see', we say when comprehension breaks. When we promise 'to take at look at' that situation, we are not necessarily expecting to scrutinise a topographical arrangement. An opinion is presented as being 'in that person's view', and indeed, if you close your eyes for a moment and think where you are you will find that picture behind your eyes. What we cannot see we imagine, and even that word comes from an image or picture. As we 'envisage' an event taking place, we 'focus' our attention on it. So we form a picture of its occurrence in our mind.

And then along come the inventors and they turn their attention to improving scientific precision through sight. This is particularly true of the medical world where enlightened minds find ways of seeing things that are otherwise invisible, and the instruments that help them to do that they generally call a '........... scope'. In the 19th century, the auroscope reflected candlelight into a mirror with a central hole, through which the operator peered to see into the ear; it had been preceded by the eye machine or opthalmoscope. Many other 'scopes' appeared; but the stethoscope which doesn't actually look, but listens, does so in order to help the practitioner build up a medical picture in his mind's eye.

All these clever people and their inventions in the cause of medicine were preceded in time and prioritised in status by Copernicus who, instead of focusing down, sought to extend his vision to the galactic bounds – and met trouble as a result.

But this suggests, in a misleading way, that seeing is the complete experience and in the Historic House we have to do an awful lot of seeing things which were not meant to be looked at exclusively. Not even the things that were designed to be beautiful – chairs, tables, candelabras – were intended to be seen without being used. They were an ideal combination. Some things were not even meant to be beautiful and kitchen things were functional only. Of course we are uneasy when we go into a Historic House kitchen which, although superficially and immediately attractive, quickly reveals itself as an uneasy conversion into a display experience. We look at the listless pattern on the wall of spirtle, bannock-turner and ladle, the copper 'batterie de cuisine', arranged with meticulous attention to gradations of size and shape and in relation to an attendant lid. Wax vegetables in casual heaps of studied exactitude are piled upon the table and no crumb, dust or speck attend the vitrified oatcakes endlessly baking in a set reminiscent of the lost city of Pompeii.

And so we look, stare, are partially informed, nudged by boredom, questioned by perplexity, and in some cases, chastised by the pursuing worksheet. And no touching.

But this urge to touch is more significant than that which can be cast as a nuisance. I am not saying it should be allowed – we should have smashes, tatters and stains in a week and very little left for next week's visitors to see – but we should try to understand this urge to touch and see what we can do to meet it.

The need to understand more, relate better and interrogate the objects is genuine and good. There is a strong bond of association which is established in infancy between ourselves and the outside world. Indeed it has been shown how many of our aptitudes and capacities are laid down in childhood, in the very early days before ever conscious memory played its part. Young babies become fascinated by a particular toy, perhaps a woolly bear. The bear is clearly special and signifies more than other toys. It could be, that in claiming so much affectionate energy, some special line of discovery, especially self discovery is going on. The child psychiatrist D. W. Winnicott says that 'from birth the human child is concerned with the problem of the relation between what is objectively perceived and what is subjectively conceived of': there is, in other words, an outer reality: the continuing person in the midst of these things. There is 'me' and 'not me'. These are two realities and they must be brought into relation with each other. Something is needed to demonstrate to the 'me' that there is a whole great world out there: to represent, as it were, the whole great world of otherness and to modify the world of endless subjectivity. The woolly bear comes to represent the external world as being apart from and negotiable by 'me'. And – in clarifying the objective world outside, so is confirmation made of the subjective world of which 'I' am the centre. This is the essential central self-affirmation, necessary to us all.

Play with this object, which Winnicott calls the 'transitional object' becomes the stimulus for creative play. The starter for cultural life. The successful transition from the subject dominated empire to subject in relation to object and external reality is the source of creative living: it is the spring of the feeling that life is worth living.

The experience of a personal psychic reality which is the basis of self, comes through objects, through the control of objects and through, as a result, the feeling of magic in discovering the separated individual and his own self-hood.

If children are going to think historically, therefore, if they are going to be so placed as to be released into imaginative, creative, and culturally developing thinking, they have to be able to be in touch with these early experiences where the object signifies, the subject is confirmed, and creativity explodes into life. As sentient intellectual people we need the proximity and direct experience of the environment to generate the opportunity for historic learning.

That is why the Trust is introducing Study Boxes to its major properties and for loan at Teachers' Resource Centres. Study Boxes are collections of objects which tell about the lifestyle and the occupations of the inhabitants of that house, above and below stairs. They are antiques but since they are not top quality they expect – and will get – strenuous handling to discover their nature and functioning. Pictures and notes supply background, the house itself is the context. Already great interest has been shown in the opportunities they hold for teaching.

And there must be schools' activities rooms in Trust properties where tables can be laid, hip baths (with or without water) tried for size, and above all, the muckle wheel made to spin again as it did in the old days in Gladstone's Land at the top of the Lawnmarket. One day when Guides were in costume and doing many of the things associated with the activities of the house, one 12 year old boy came to the spinner, busy at the muckle wheel. Bit by bit she taught him how to spin and when he had learned, he returned with some friends to teach them too. Proud of their achievement they brought their families to see – the crowd about the wheel became quite dense.

Recently the British Museum laid on an exhibition 'The Human Touch' and Victoria Neumark reviewing it in the Times Education Supplement wrote: 'what an amazing force one primitive sense, touch, has for us human beings . . . the pieces seem to come alive at the touch'. Whether the curator had read his Bertrand Russell or not I do not know: but even if he had not, he knew that senses are incomplete in the information that they give and that others have to be called upon to supplement the experience and to kindle the imagination.

Thomas Hardy has a good poem about the way in which old things can signify and how imagination catches their story:
I see the hands of generations
That owned each shiny familiar thing
In play, on its knobs and indentations
And with its ancient fashioning

Still dallying:
Hands behind hands, growing paler and paler
As in a mirror a candleflame
Shows images of itself, each frailer
As it recedes, though the eye may flame
Its shape the same.

Secondly: Historic Houses are about places. Colin Ward, that trenchant writer about environmental education, recalls 'Topofilia' as being literally love of the place. Lots of places for us are childhood places – the kind of place that was prodigal, in its provision of facilities for play, the beach, the burn, the garden where the gold of autumn burnished

Schools project 'Situation Vacant', Culzean Castle, Ayrshire.

the memory and the fruits were mellow and our peace of mind complete. The experience of place is person centred – where we learn because we can't do other than absorb and enlarge and enrich and expand. And at the centre is a person or persons by whom it is cherished and who is an accepting and approving presence.

Feelings about a place do need time and no interruption to grow down. Many Houses are in beautiful settings which need to be explored. But exploration although it may need to be guided should not tolerate control – exploration means that group of children in the National Gallery – who nobody was controlling and who did not need it either. Sometimes a graceful retreat on the part of the teacher leaves people be to discover their environment and themselves to relate to it and we should sometimes take a look at our urge to assume command.

Recently we were given the opportunity to work with Historic Buildings and Monuments in Scotland on the preparation of a Young Person's Guide to Stirling Castle. The task was intimidating because here of all places it would be inappropriate to interrupt the impact of this noble accumulation of history, and of the growth of the ancient buildings from the elemental rock with the twittering of worksheets and questionnaires. Any Young Person's Guide must release rather than control and this was how, when at Culloden, the Academy VIth year produced a collage for the Trust's Visitor Centre there, it drew for its inspiration on the desolating experience of Drumossie Moor itself; and it carried within itself this vital link of communication.

There is another lighter side, however. Much associated with the wearing of the plaid youngsters go to Culloden to discover how it is done. Meeting for the first time this great length of material (woven to the pattern of a fragment left behind on the battlefield) they try to manage it and to adjust it to their person by arranging it in pleats on the floor and lying on it and fastening it about their person. Even so clear a sense of place as Culloden and the reminiscence that hits us all can make its own most cheerful provision.

Thus, the muckle wheel and the plaid. What of the souter?

Everyone knows he's a shoemaker. The National Trust for Scotland has Souter Johnnie's Cottage in Ayrshire. Children come to work with the souter, to help to repair their own shoes and to handle the quaint instruments that he uses to do it. But the person of the souter was more than the living embodiment of the craftsman of old: he is the mediator through whom the ancient skills were opened up and the intricacies of the use of specific tools for the trade. Through that present day souter, children learned how people lived and what they did and his role as the souter was to relate to the children, a task more important and more demanding even than his own skills with his equipment and mended shoes. It was the character of the old man that the children would not forget, and his friendly interest in his visitors and his concern that they should understand and experience the appeal of his craft.

All Houses need their people to act as their mediators or their interpreters. They do not necessarily have to be craftsmen to do it. We expect them, rightly, to be informed and to have their information ordered in their mind and presented clearly. Most Houses are working at ensuring that that information is around and available.

But there is something else which is more elusive and more important. No matter how beautiful, how packed with history and with fine objects, how magic in its appeal, all these things will be of no account if the people that we meet there do not give us the kind of attention and warmth that makes us know we are welcome.

The real visit, the one where learning can take place, is the one where welcome is assured and warmth and personal attention assure us that we signify.

Now, to teach information and to have it available is one thing. But, to talk about communication skills, the intuitive arts of the person to person approach – that is something again. In fact it has occupied some of us more than a year or two to analyse, study, assess the task of the Guide in the Historic House and to seek to provide. That is how the Insite Project has come into being and because we are dealing with a skill that rests with persons, we are constructing a training programme around a team of Consultants who will work on a person to person basis. No superimposed standardised formula would work here. We deal with individual properties and with individuals who work with them and we are grateful to the Carnegie UK Trust for funding a pilot programme in Lothian, Fife and Borders to enable us to work in Houses both in private ownership and in the care of the Trust on this project.

Of course, Insite is for everybody that comes. And equally, it is for those who in some ways make the more exacting demands on our guiding staff – the young people. Exacting in that we know that our goal, as we said at the outset is enjoyment, absorption and the spirit of enquiry – and that it takes one wrong-footed guide to assassinate that and to impose a regulatory attitude onto a visiting group or an individual child. Guides who do such an exacting task need to be assured of support, back up, guidance, training and the availability of regular consultation. Children are the most significant section of the market.

At the outset I mentioned the Sandford Award, one of whose criteria for winning is the imaginative use of the property. Some applicants for next year's Award are working specifically on the development of these three aspects on which I have spoken: contents, place and people. Properties who use worksheets may apply – and those with a souter, a plaid or a muckle wheel – or something – stand an even better chance.

A selection of resource materials
from independent museums.

Resources Development in Independent Museums

Rob Shorland-Ball

Rob Shorland-Ball is Honorary Secretary of the Association of Independent Museums and Director of the Museum of East Anglian Life at Stowmarket in Suffolk. He changed from a teaching career in Yorkshire to become Curator of Worsbrough Mill Museum, Barnsley in 1975 and was subsequently County Museums Officer for South Yorkshire until 1981.

Why resources development in *independent* museums? Before answering that question perhaps it would be useful to explain the term 'independent' museum. An independent museum is one funded partly or wholly by other than local authority or national monies. In many cases it may enjoy 'mixed economy' funding with some underpinning of local authority finance being supplemented by earned income from admission fees and shop trading. The distinction, then, between independent and other museums is, at least as far as this paper is concerned, one of management structure. Is there, perhaps, a doubt in some minds that such museums have an education service? Well, of course some do not but all – even those more chimerical ones like the 'Museum of the Unrealised Idea' – can, and do, provide an educational resource. May I suggest, then, that the management structure of the museum is less important in the context of this publication than the educational resources it can provide.

I was interested to hear in Gordon Kirk's paper of 'the progressive consensus'. What a splendid term with which to brow-beat reactionary colleagues! I am sure that the progressive consensus still espouses the cause of 'child-centred' education. It seems logical, then, to base what follows on the experiences of a typical child consumer visiting a museum.

I am sure you are all familiar with the large envelopes, often beautifully inscribed, which may arrive after a school visit to a museum containing 'thank you' letters. Some such letters are clearly teacher-inspired and very conventional in layout and content. Others, written from the heart, are freer in expression, sometimes sternly admonitory and critical, often entertaining and always useful because they represent a consumer reaction to the services we provide.

There follows just such a letter – contrived only to the extent that it represents an amalgam of some of the best and the worst received at the Museum of East Anglian Life this season. Spelling and punctuation in such letters are often at variance with accepted standards but I have not attempted to make deliberate mistakes in what follows. I treasure such gems as the letter addressed to the Museum of East *Anglican* Life which started 'Dear Curate' or another, a poem to our 1 tonne Suffolk Punch horse, Remus, who stands some 16 hands high. The first line was 'Oh Remus, your . . .' and then followed a great scratching out as the poet, seeking the correct adjective to qualify the word 'form' – 'Oh Remus, your . . . form' – attempted variant spellings of both 'fairy' and 'furry' to obtain the desired cadence.

Before moving to the letter I should briefly explain what there is to see at the Museum of East Anglian Life. The site, extending over 70 acres of attractive Suffolk countryside includes several re-erected buildings – a smithy, a watermill, a windpump – working exhibits such as steam engines and the Suffolk Punch Remus as well as conventional museum displays on domestic life, farming and industry in the area. In June 1986, HRH The Duke of Gloucester opened a major new building including craft workshops, video interpretation and working machines. There are several references to the new building in the letter which follows. The Museum has an important education service run by a seconded teacher from a well-equipped classroom on site; a mobile museum goes out to schools as part of an outreach programme.

* * *

Dear Curator of the Museum,

Your mobile van visited our School and was good with all the things and the slides in colour. Mr. Davies said we could go to see your Museum and we went on Tuesday. We brought back all the things you had lent us to learn from in our School. Mr. Davies said I could carry the corn stick and it was heavy But I felt like an old farmer walking along with it.

I liked your horse. Mr. Davies gave him a sugar lump and he nearly bit his finger. The boy showed us Remus' harness and put it on; we saw him pull a cart.

The exhibitions were really good; I liked the gypsy caravan and the old fashioned parlour. There was too much dust on the table; it should be polished Mr. Davies said. In the new building we saw a video of a basket maker and we talked to the wheel maker man. He helped us with our work-sheet because he knew all the answers he said. I liked his coffin. There was a film show upstairs but the man in the coat with the radio on him said it was not working. But he did make the big steam engine work and he told off Mr. Davies for getting in the engine.

Then the museum teacher Miss Spurling said come to her class-room which she had on the Museum. Darren Wainwright scraped his chair on the floor twice and Miss Spurling made him the dunce when she was making an old time lesson. We heard a tape recording of an old lady talking about when she was at school; you could not hear the words and I pretended I was Remus.

Going to the Tea Room for our picnic I saw the watermill, some ducks and a rabbit. And the toilets, we had to wait in the ladies and Mr. Davies said come on but we could not wait.

I liked the Shop too; it was full of things. I bought a postcard and a pencil and a book of the Museum. The Kit Kat was bent and sticky by the heat; it was horrid.

I liked the action in the Museum and the workmen and all the old things. The coach was in the car park and we went back.

With love from
Amanda

*   *   *

Clearly there is much here to enjoy – and clearly Amanda enjoyed her visit – but there is also much to learn. In the particular museum receiving the letter, the problems of the unpolished table, the queue in the ladies loo, the bent and sticky Kit-Kat and the film show which does not work all require specific attention.

In the wider field of education resources in independent museums or, indeed, any museums, Amanda's letter may serve as a paradigm for what resources school visitors might hope to find.

Amanda mentioned, in no particular order, a number of factors which had impressed her during her visit. They may be summarised under three heads:

(a) Visitor services
(b) Specific education provision
(c) The museum experience.

(a) Visitor services
In the context of our proceedings visitor services may not seem very important but they may make or mar a visit. The coach park, the toilets, the tea room and the shop all have their rôles to play. The museum shop, particularly, may be a valuable educational resource in its own right.[1] In the first instance, for very young children, it may provide an opportunity for shopping and handling money in a 'protected' environment. The good museum shop

should also sell useful items, be they simple souvenirs, or booklets, replicas and models which extend the parameters of the educational visit. Sadly, however, some museum shops are not good. They stock 'tat' and because visiting school children with 'spending money' burning their pockets are not discriminating shoppers, such shops sell 'tat' too. Here, though, is an area where teachers can be a powerful influence for good in influencing the stock purchases for museum shops. Make plain to the offending museum – preferably in a letter – why you consider the shop to be a poor one. And actively discourage or even prevent school parties in your care from visiting an unsatisfactory shop during your visit. To see 30 or more lots of 'spending money' going out of the museum gate unspent is a sobering experience for any museum which enjoys an income from its shop.

(b) Education provisions
Then there are the specific *education provisions*. Amanda mentioned a mobile museum, a loan service, visual aids, worksheets, an Education Centre classroom and an Education Officer – 'the Museum teacher Miss Spurling said come to her classroom which she had on the Museum'.

Not every museum can muster these resources but nearly all have some, some have most and a good number of the larger museums have them all. Some analyses of museum education provision have been carried out[2] but it is sad that the Museums Association's *Museums Yearbook* does not include any details of such provision in museum entries (other than where a specific education officer or section is listed).

Outreach – taking the museum to the

children – is particularly important and rewarding but it is very expensive in staff time and in what the Army knows as matériel – the equipment necessary to provide such a service. To be parochial for a moment: we operate a mobile museum service at Stowmarket taking an 8′ × 25′ converted mobile library out to schools for a week at a time. The vehicle contains an introductory exhibition reflecting the range and scope of the main museum's collections and displays. It carries a number of related handling items and a tape-slide programme which can be used in the Mobile or taken into the classroom. Teachers find a Mobile visit invaluable before a school party visit to the main museum. It performs a valuable introductory rôle, it introduces artefacts in the familiar classroom environment and it de-mystifies The Museum (capital T, capital M) in the eyes of those children who may never have visited a museum before.

There is much more to be said about specific education provision on the museum site but I will mention only two other aspects and those briefly.

The good museum education officer, on site and knowing the collections is an invaluable resource. Such a one may prove a veritable lighthouse of learning to the busy school teacher with too little time to prepare adequately a visit to a large and educationally very rich collection or museum.

And yet . . . and yet, the school teacher knows his or her pupils and should know what she/he wants to achieve from the visit. There is no substitute for adequate preparation for a visit and the good education officer may be more valuable in preparing the visit with the teacher rather than actually working with the children.

Which brings me to the worksheet. You will have already read the amusing account by Marista Leishman of a conversion on the road to the National Gallery in respect of worksheets. I am still very ambivalent; I believe they can be a valuable tool and that they have their place but they should not entirely replace the teacher working with the children and the children discovering for themselves. Remember Amanda's letter? '. . . the wheel maker man.' (He) helped us with our worksheet because he knew all the answers he said'. How often does the well intentioned (but badly trained) demonstrator or attendant provide 'all the answers' because he does, indeed, know them by heart.

(c) The 'museum experience'

And finally *'the museum experience'* – that above all is what we are all about.

In a splendid piece of late Victorian moralising Thomas Greenwood wrote in *Museums and Galleries* (1888):

'. . . knowledge . . . should give an infinitely higher and more reverential feeling of the Almighty.'

A difficult concept to impart to a visiting 10-year old but implicit there is the 'specialness' of museums. 'The sense sublime of something far more deeply interfused' that Wordsworth saw in the natural world is inherent in the collections of *real* objects that are the raison d'être of museums. See the wonder and the comprehension in a child's eyes (or those of an adult too) when its thumb fits exactly into the thumb print of a Roman potter, petrified for all time in the base of a simple pot. Amanda again:

'. . . Mr. Davies said I could carry the corn stick and it was heavy. But I felt like an old farmer walking along with it . . .'

and

'. . . I liked your horse . . .'

and

'. . . I liked the action in the Museum and the workmen and all the old things . . .'

Even the smallest, crudest, simplest museum houses real things so different from the second-hand, two-dimensional experiences which we feed on so avidly from television and cinema screen. Many museums, and especially the smaller independents, do not have elaborate education services and provisions but they all have one inimitable resource on which teachers can draw: they can offer, through their collections, the experience of an historical reality.

I wrote to several independent museums when I knew I was to write this paper enquiring about their educational resources. I was overwhelmed with magnificent published material, with slides and with long and helpful letters.

In all I contacted 14 museums and all responded. All had teachers' packs, most had worksheets, 7 had special education centres, 8 had specialist education staff and all but one clearly placed great emphasis on their work with schools.

Writing in the *Museums Journal* in December 1980, Professor Brian Lewis noted:

'. . . even the smallest museums tend to house collections which are, in certain important respects, the best of their kind – and . . . the largest museums tend to house collections which may be 'without parallel' (in terms of value, uniqueness, comprehensiveness etc.) anywhere else in the world. . . .'[3]

He neatly summarises the significance of museums as an educational resource. Like a rich lode the resource is there to be mined. Many of the larger, richer or more enlightened museums take their educational resources seriously and provide a variety of services to enhance and complement the resource. Where there are no services the resource still remains and then teachers themselves must be their own miners, working the lode for the benefit of their pupils.

Sources

1.   David Sekers, 'The Educational Potential of the Museum Shop', *Museums Journal* Vol. 76, No. 4, March 1977.

2.   Jeffrey Taylor, 'Primary Education and Local Museums in Cumbria, *Museums Journal* Vol. 84, No. 3, December 1984; Department of Education and Science, *A Survey of the Use Some Hertfordshire Schools Make of Museum Services,* London, 1986.

3.   Brian N. Lewis, 'The Museum as an Educational Facility', *Museums Journal* Vol. 80, No. 3, December 1980.

APPENDIX
Educational Visits to Museums

Museum Visits and the Curriculum

This indicates the broad stages in planning a museum visit. It is based on the view that school visits to museums, spread over the whole year, should have a direct educational benefit – that they should further the broad aims and objectives of the school curriculum and link specifically with the class syllabus. In doing so, over and above the acquisition of knowledge, visits will be concerned with developing specific skills, ideas and concepts and providing a range of experiences – aesthetic, ethical, spiritual, creative. By contrast 'outings' or 'treats' are of limited educational value.

Most benefit can be obtained from a museum visit if there is:

concentration on a definite theme(s) closely integrated with school work;

careful structuring of the work;

an enquiry-based approach.

More specific aims and format will vary with the age/ability of the pupils, but generally speaking younger children will appreciate a broad look at a topic. P6–S1 will benefit from more direct investigation and older pupils from an increased awareness of the value of evidence and how we learn.

Organisation

Arrangements for visits to museums, art galleries, zoos or historic houses are essentially the same as for any out-of-school visit.

Teachers should refer to their own education authority's guidelines to check on local requirements relating to eg safety, staff-pupil ratios, excursion grants, parental consent.

A. Planning the Visit

1. *Link Curriculum and Resources.*
   Check early with the museum that there is enough relevant material to make a visit with pupils worthwhile. The museum should be considered along with a range of other likely resources when you are planning your broad scheme of work for the year. Other resources might include museum loan kits, travelling exhibitions, schools broadcasts and LEA Resource Centres.

2. *Teacher's Preparatory visit to the Museum*
   a. Select the parts of the displays or temporary exhibitions you wish to use; discuss requirements with museum staff (objects for handling, short talk/AV presentation, the contribution of museum education staff and class teacher).

   b. Anticipate difficulties – eg congestion and need for small groups, poor visibility, labelling and language difficulties.

   c. Assess teaching techniques and

materials you could use on the visit, how you would divide up the time . . . and the pupils.

d. Begin preparation of worksheets/ workcards, as appropriate.

e. Check availability of eg clipboards, stools/cushions, toilets, cloakrooms, refreshments, facilities for handicapped, parking.

3. *Booking the Class Visit*

a. Bookings should normally be made at least 2 weeks in advance. Otherwise difficulties can be caused for the museum concerned and booked groups may already be at work in your chosen area.

b. When making bookings, please supply the museum with the following information:
date(s) required;
time of arrival;
approximate length of stay;
parts of museum to be used;
topic to be studied;
name of teacher-in-charge;
name and telephone number of school;
class and number of pupils to visit (max. − single class size);
number of teachers/adults (1:12 pupils for preference);
whether clipboards/cushions/stools etc. required (if available);
It would be useful to state alternative dates/times in case the museum is already fully booked.

c. Bear in mind other organisational points − eg transport, costings, permission, insurance cover, packed lunches.

4. *Class Preparation*

Class preparation is essential to the success of a visit. Not only should the visit form part of the overall curricular programme, but a period or two immediately before the visit can deal more directly with:

a. New vocabulary and concepts to be met with at the museum;

b. 'Why we go to museums' and 'what we do when we get there' (perhaps with an explanation of a layout of the museum/ gallery);

c. The need for responsible behaviour in the museum − museums are exciting places but not funfairs;

d. Last minute details for pupils − eg transport, packed lunches, clothing, money.

B. At the Museum

1. *The Learning Experience*

Whether led by the class teacher or the museum teacher, this will normally include:
group talk and discussion amongst the exhibits;
individual investigations, probably with worksheets.

It may also include the handling of objects, the showing of a few selected slides or the relevant part of a film or filmstrip and an opportunity for pupils to look at what excites their interest outside the formal structure of the experience.

Remember, however, that the unique aspect of museums, galleries, zoos etc. is their collections − the 'objects'. Time in the museum should centre on the objects, rather than on work that could just as well be carried out at school. Pupils might be encouraged to use cameras, cassette-recorders, or sketchbooks as a means of collecting evidence for follow-up work.

2. *The Role of the Teacher*

The class teacher will normally work alongside the museum staff where present. Otherwise, the class teacher (together with accompanying adults) will be responsible for all the teaching and supervision.

Worksheets and workcards can be of real value for personal investigation by pupils but it is helpful to remember that pupils may often concentrate on written questions to the virtual exclusion of the objects. A teacher will want therefore, to monitor each small group of pupils in turn;

discuss and expand on the content of the questions;

encourage pupils to look closely, see how things are made, from what, for what purposes, how they relate;

encourage them to question and seek answers that are based on evidence in the museum;

encourage pupils to follow up investigations and researches at school and at home.

One lengthy, unbroken worksheet will encourage congestion and confusion. In order to spread groups of 3/4 pupils around the work area, it is preferable to have several short worksheets, or a single one clearly subdivided. Not all groups will necessarily cover all the ground, but they can report back to each other in class as part of the follow-up.

C. After the Visit

1. *Follow-up and Evaluation*

Further work in the classroom or return visits to the museum or other locations (eg local buildings, archives departments, library services) are related to the initial investigations in the museum. At this stage, museum loan kits might be used where available.

Pupils, when they return to the classroom, should collate and discuss with the teachers the evidence collected during their investigations. They should determine how their findings are to be presented for display and discussion in the classroom, eg through drawings and paintings, creative writing, tape/slide presentations, role-playing, classroom collections, three-dimensional models, etc.

Subsequent discussion and reporting-back procedures, based upon the classroom displays, should include evaluation of whether the visit achieved its intended educational purpose. Pupils should be encouraged to look critically at the process of learning. At this stage, pupils might identify future areas of investigation. A 'thank you' letter from pupils to individual museum staff and an invitation to visit the school might be considered.

2. *Evaluation*

Evaluation of the success of the visit should be attempted at different levels:

did the pupils enjoy the visit?
do they want to go back to the museum?
was it stimulating for staff – or a strain?
did it contribute as intended to the course and curriculum?
was the planning satisfactory – school, transport, museum?
was the museum helpful, welcoming, effective?
was the museum satisfied with the arrangements?
was the visit 'cost-effective'?
would you go back with the same/another class?
what changes would you make in future visits?

Museums generally welcome teachers' impressions of the visit. These can help them considerably with their future educational work.

The text of this Appendix is taken from the Scottish Museums Council's publication *A Directory Museum Education Scotland* with some revision (Edinburgh, 1981). Copies of the publication are available from HMSO and all good bookshops.

Information for visitors to museums, art galleries and historic houses in Scotland can be readily obtained from the Scottish Museums Council's *Scottish Museums and Galleries Guide* (Edinburgh, 1986). Copies of the Guide are available from all good bookshops.

Dd. 0287052 C12·5 9/87 McC.